the who

BY CHRIS CHARLESWORTH

Edited by Andrew King
Cover & Book designed by 4i
Picture research by Chris Charlesworth

ISBN: 0.7119.4306.0 Order No: OP 47740

Exclusive Distributors
Book Sales Limited, 8/9 Frith Street, London W1V 5TZ, UK.
Music Sales Corporation, 257 Park Avenue South, New York, NY 10010, USA.
Music Sales Pty Limited, 120 Rothschild Avenue, Rosebery, NSW 2018, Australia.

To the Music Trade only:
Music Sales Limited, 8/9 Frith Street, Lond-

Photo credit:
Harry Goodwin: ii, 13, 20, 34, 41, 80, 89; Dezo Hoffm
Barry Plummer: back cover, 2,3,4, 5, 6, 7, 8, iv, 33, 35, 57, €

Every effort has been made to trace the copyright holders
two were unreachable. We would be grateful if the phot

Printed in the United Kingdom by Ebenezer Bay

A catalogue record for this book is available

OMNIBUS PRESS
LONDON · NEW YORK · SYDNEY

CONTENTS

INTRODUCTION

The Who's forté was always the live stage, but along the way they made some pretty decent records too, as well as a few duffers. Like all those rare bands who met as teenagers and managed to stay together through thick and thin, playing on stage became second nature to them – at least when they did it regularly – and on their best nights a sixth sense seemed to take over the tiller and lead them and their audiences towards a kind of rock heaven that most bands can only dream about.

For the first ten years of their career they probably played more live shows than any other band of their era but, relatively speaking, they were never prolific recording-wise. In the Sixties, while The Beatles put out 10 studio albums and The Rolling Stones eight, The Who managed only four. Nowadays this miserly output is all too common among established acts, but back then top bands were expected to release an album a year and a few non-album singles while touring constantly, so even though The Who's output matched present day standards, they were still under-achievers compared to their peers.

They didn't really speed up in the Seventies either, with just four more studio albums, a live set and a collection of unreleased outtakes. That said, there's still a total of just over 200 extant recorded songs credited to The Who over the best part of 20 years, a substantial body of work by anybody's standards. Unfortunately there have been far too many unimaginative Who compilations along the way, which has resulted in only a small percentage of their total output being widely known. This is a great

shame, because there's far more depth and enjoyment to be found in The Who's catalogue than 'My Generation', 'Pinball Wizard', 'Won't Get Fooled Again' and the half-dozen or so other Who classics that are endlessly recycled by most radio stations.

One of the reasons for The Who's relative under-achievement in the studio was the court settlement awarded to Shel Talmy who produced their first three singles and all of their first LP. After a bitter legal dispute, Talmy and The Who parted company but the American producer was awarded a substantial royalty on all their work up to and including 'Who's Next'. The Who therefore found themselves in an ironic position: the more successful they became and the more records they sold, the more they enriched their worst enemy. It was financially crippling for them insofar as they never earned a just reward from record sales during the period when they sold most records. That's reason enough to limit your output and play live as often as possible (Talmy, of course, received zilch from live shows), but the whole awful business doubtless shaped the direction that The Who's career took for the next 15 years.

At first, like all their peers, The Who were a 'singles' band – there was no other type of band in 1965 and '66 – and most of their terrific early singles, none of which made any real impact in the US, weren't taken from concurrent albums as singles are today. Consequently, because it is album based rather than strictly chronological, many of their better known early songs don't appear in this analysis until the later chapter on compilations, most of them under 'Meaty Beaty Big And Bouncy'.

Last year The Who received the box-set treatment with '30 Years Of Maximum R&B', a well received 4CD retrospective of 79 mostly remastered tracks compiled by myself. At the time of going to press The Who's record companies were embarking gingerly on a wholesale repackaging programme of The Who's entire back catalogue which will hopefully result in bonus tracks being added to CD albums in order to bring up the running time from around 40 minutes to over an hour.

My thanks to John Atkins, Melissa & Gary Hurley and Ed Hanel for their help and insights into The Who's music. A few quotes have been taken from interviews with the band over the years and from Dave Marsh's excellent Who biography *Before I Get Old*. Fans of The Who seeking a forum for discussion and an exchange of ideas and opinions are directed to *Generations* magazine, c/o Phil Hopkins, 1 Egbert Rd, Meols, Wirral, Merseyside, England, L47 5AH. In the first issue of *Generations* Hopkins' co-editor John Atkins wrote that The Who were... 'loud, brash, hard, noisy, fast and exciting, but also subtle, complex, intelligent, imaginative, and profound."

I couldn't agree more.

Chris Charlesworth, September 1994

All songs written by Pete Townshend unless otherwise stated.

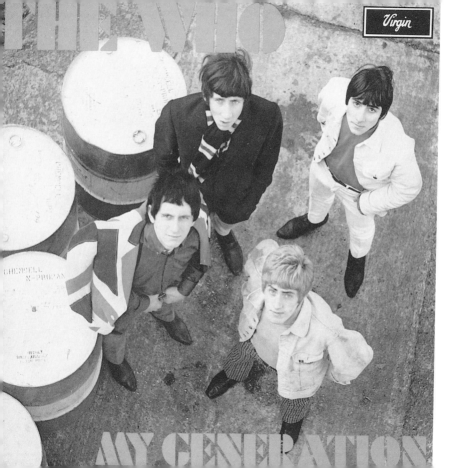

MY GENERATION

ORIGINAL UK ISSUE: BRUNSWICK RECORDS LAT 8616, RELEASED DECEMBER 1965; RE-ISSUED ON VIRGIN V2179, OCTOBER, 1980. US: DECCA DL 4664 (MONO), DL 74664 (STEREO); CD: MCA 31330.

The songs that appeared on The Who's début album were recorded at IBC Studios in London's Upper Regent Street in October and November of 1965. At the controls was Shel Talmy, an American expatriate record producer who had already recorded two hit singles with the group – 'I Can't Explain' and 'Anyway Anyhow Anywhere' – but whose relationship with them, especially with Pete Townshend and co-manager Kit Lambert, was rapidly deteriorating.

At the end of 1964 Lambert, desperate to get The Who on record, signed them to a niggardly production deal that empowered Talmy to place the group's records with whatever record company he chose, always assuming that some company some-where wanted The Who on their label. Talmy took The Who's tapes to American Decca, with whom he had good contacts, who in turn released The Who's records in the UK on Brunswick. Both 'Explain' and 'Anyway' had been respectable Top Ten hits but Lambert and Townshend had reached the conclusion that they could produce The Who's music better than Talmy. They wanted out but were locked into a deal that last-ed for five years. Soon they would take drastic measures to dump Talmy which in the long term proved financially disastrous for them, but in the meantime there was the first album to record with him whether they liked it or not.

Initially the first LP was to have been predominantly R&B covers which The Who per-formed live on stage, but as the project developed and Pete Townshend wrote more and more original material for the group, the album settled into an explosive mix of covers and Townshend originals.

Few albums have been so crunchingly influential. Scores of noisy bands that followed have cited The Who's début as their inspiration. Indeed, the interplay between Moon's crashing drums (this album demonstrates unequivocally that Moon was far and away the most imaginative and talented young drummer in England) and Entwistle's super-speed trebly bass, Townshend's ringing chords and use of the guitar as a sonic tool rather than a melodic instrument, and Daltrey's truculent vocal attack, was quite unlike anything else around at the time. Special mention is due to Nicky Hopkins, the session pianist, who was brought in to help fill out The Who's sound but managed to sound like a fully paid-up member of the band, no mean achievement in a quartet as combative as The Who at this stage in their evolution.

The record was released in December 1965 in a sleeve featuring a bird's eye view of the four members of The Who gazing skywards, a pose that Blondie copied in an almost perfect (there were five of them) pastiche 12 years later. In the US, where American Decca released the album in April of 1966, the title was changed to 'The Who Sing My Generation' and, in an attempt to jump on the British Invasion bandwagon, the cover shot featured The Who with Big Ben in the background. Although the Americans didn't realise it at the time, it was particularly appropriate in view of the 'Englishness' for which The Who would eventually become known.

It reached number five in the UK charts but flopped in the US. Polydor UK has never owned the rights to the 'My Generation' LP which was reissued by Virgin at the beginning of the Eighties but deleted when vinyl became obsolete. Consequently the only CD of 'My Generation' extant is the US MCA version which in the UK can be found only at limited outlets as a pricey import.

OUT IN THE STREET

A flamenco-like guitar flourish in the style that Pete used on several early Who songs opens this spiky, jerked up rocker that sets the stage for what was termed 'Maximum Rhythm & Blues' on the famous poster advertising their Marquee shows. On the circuit The Who began by playing R&B covers but with the ammunition at their disposal the songs metamorphosed into a fairly brutal style of rock and 'Out In The Street' exemplifies this. Nothing to do with the Bruce Springsteen song of the same name, but the lyrics carry a similar message: Don't Mess With Us.

I DON'T MIND
(Brown)

Slow, soulful blues seems at odds with the violent attack of songs like 'My Generation' but this is the material that Roger liked to sing. Although his pitching isn't perfect, the band create just the right atmosphere, tense and moody throughout. There's a great little guitar flourish at the end of the solo.

THE GOOD'S GONE

A cheerless, forbidding song, definitely the moodiest song on the album, taken at a deliberate pace with Roger adopting an uncharacteristically deep voice. If The Who's intention was to create an air of misery, they succeeded admirably. Hopkins' piano and Keith's drums duel away in the background.

LA LA LA LIES

An attractive melody is given greater emphasis by Keith who restricts himself to just tom-toms on the verse and chorus, an unusual arrangement for the time. Only on the middle eight and solo is he allowed to crash his cymbals. Shel Talmy released this track as a single without The Who's consent and it might even have been a hit had it not been in competition with the far superior 'Happy Jack'.

MUCH TOO MUCH

Fairly standard beat group fare of the period, enlivened – as ever – by Keith's drumming and Roger's loutish vocal delivery in which he rejects his girl for displaying feelings too deep for him to reciprocate, probably a common enough state of affairs for Roger at the time.

MY GENERATION

If 'My Generation' was the only record The Who had ever recorded, they would still deserve an honourable mention in any history of rock. Their third single, *the* Mod anthem of 1965, is still the best known song in their entire catalogue. Pete Townshend has often regretted penning the memorable lines 'Hope I die before I get old' but 'My Generation' remains the hardest hitting single released by any UK pop group in 1965. The Beatles and the Stones, remember, were still writing love songs at the time this was released.

'Generation' started life as a slow blues, not unlike the version that The Who

would often play in concert during the Seventies. Then Kit Lambert suggested Pete speed things up. Just before it was released as a single – at the suggestion of co-manager Chris Stamp – Roger was fired from the band for his violent attacks on the other three. He was quickly re-instated when 'Generation' leapt up the charts and its success undoubtedly saved Roger from a life as a tearaway – and The Who from extinction.

It's a cataclysmic *tour de force*, from Roger's 'controversial' stuttering vocals to John's lumpy bass solo, from Pete's grungy two chord guitar riff to Keith's by now regular assault on the drums, and its rebellious stance was a perfect war cry for anyone under 20 who felt that the grown-up world just wasn't for them. As if the first two raging minutes weren't enough, The Who pile on the pressure with an upward key change and climax with a brutal wipe-out of distorted feed-back and general mayhem.

'My Generation' reached number two in the UK charts, the highest position any Who single would ever achieve. The fact that 'The Carnival Is Over' by The Seekers kept it from reaching the top may have terminally affected Pete's attitude towards the charts – probably for the better in the long run. It didn't chart at all in the US.

THE KIDS ARE ALRIGHT

Another Mod anthem, nowhere near as brutal as 'Generation' but equally as haunting in different ways. Opening with a lovely chord flourish – by now a Who trademark – and based around Townshend's favourite jangly A and D chords, 'Kids' is as melodic as any track on the album, even Beatlish in concept, but again it's Keith's enormous drumming that drives the song to its many crescendos. Perhaps the most impressive section in the whole piece is the guitar solo, more slashing chords that reach a stupendous clanging climax, all underpinned by Keith, giving Pete and Roger a launchpad into the final verse that all of Britain's serious up and coming guitarists must have envied.

Most of this wonderful solo was edited out when the album was released in the US. Not until the release of The Who's 4CD box set was the unedited version officially released there.

PLEASE PLEASE PLEASE
(Brown, Terry)

In which Roger emotes in true James Brown fashion and the band back-up staccato style. Actually, Roger squeezes everything he can from Brown's tear-jerker, grossly overdoing it in the process but the song is saved by Pete's lively but rambling blues solo. This one might have worked live but on record everyone seems to try too hard with disappointing results.

IT'S NOT TRUE

With a lighter touch than the rest of the album, 'It's Not True' approaches the typical beat group sound of the Sixties, but with The Who's rhythm section pounding away, it's a far cry from Merseybeat. Keith, in particular, excels on an upbeat song in which Roger denies a variety of slanderous rumours about his shady past, most of which probably were true.

I'M A MAN
(McDaniel)

Bo Diddley's lurching blues standard became a *tour de force* in the hands of The Who, with Roger's macho attack perfect for its strutting delivery. Pete wades into a lengthy solo complete with volume control feedback 'freakout effects', all the while duelling with Nicky Hopkins' more tastefully played piano. Effectively, they turn the second half of the song into a fiery instrumental showcase.

'I'm A Man' did not appear on the US LP and is not on the MCA CD. However, it does appear on the US album 'Two's Missing' (see below).

A LEGAL MATTER

A nagging little riff underpins a song about divorce – hardly common material for pop songwriters in 1965 – which is given a keen edge by the knowledge that Roger had indeed suffered the slings and arrows of marital breakdown by this time. Perhaps that's why Pete sings lead over Nicky Hopkins' piano. Clearly influenced by the Stones, especially 'The Last Time' which it resembles in many respects, Shel Talmy chose to release 'Legal Matter' as a single without The Who's consent, but it only reached Number 32.

THE OX
(Townshend, Entwistle, Moon, Hopkins)

The closing instrumental is a far cry from the kind of melodic efforts recorded by 'instrumental' groups like The Shadows or, indeed, any 'instrumental' band of the day. Keith's relentless tom-tom barrage carries the music throughout, but the featured instruments are Pete's abandoned guitar slashes and Nicky Hopkins' piano, with John's menacing bass acting as a counterpoint rumble from somewhere deep within. 'Wipeout' by The Safaris is the logical touchstone for Keith, who always was a huge fan of surf music and its rolling drum style, but there the surfing allusion stops. 'The Ox' is actually a 12-bar blues but it has no real melody in the accepted sense of the term, just the bass riff, and a brutal onslaught which at times teeters on the edge of musical anarchy, at least for its time.

Pete: "In the studio it was possible – with a bit of frigging around – to get the sound and energy we had on stage, and this is the first Who record where we really caught that. Because this is an instrumental, what you get is The Band, the sound of this tremendous machine working almost by itself, that incredible chemistry we had in The Who, and that we kept right up until Keith Moon dropped dead."

Listening to Keith here, it's a wonder he didn't drop dead from exhaustion after the session.

A QUICK ONE

ORIGINAL UK ISSUE: REACTION 593 002, RELEASED DECEMBER 1966; UK CD: POLYDOR 835 728-24.
US: DECCA DL 4892 (MONO), DL 74892 (STEREO), CD: MCAD 31331.

By the time The Who came to record their second album they were skint through smashing up too much expensive gear, so their music publisher suggested that if each member of the group contributed at least two songs the publishers would advance £500 to each member, a considerable sum in 1966. The offer was accepted and Daltrey, Entwistle and Moon were sent off with pens in their hands to compose songs.

Creatively speaking, it was an absurd idea, especially at a time when Townshend was writing material of the calibre of 'Substitute' and 'Happy Jack', and the album suffers as a result. It's a rag-bag of styles of variable quality, lacking cohesion and any real sense of purpose. Townshend's compositions are infinitely better than anything else on the album, especially 'So Sad About Us' and the second half of 'A Quick One', though Entwistle turned in his first great Who song, 'Boris The Spider'. Even the most charitable fans must have scratched their heads at Moon and Daltrey's contributions.

The album was again recorded largely at IBC Studios during November of 1966, and released the following month in the UK where it made number 4 in the LP chart. In America it was retitled 'Happy Jack' after the single that was added at the expense of 'Heatwave', coming out in May of the following year but failing to chart. Apparently the Americans felt 'A Quick One' was too risqué for an LP title.

RUN RUN RUN

A heavy sounding fuzztone bass riff opens The Who's second LP, suggesting – wrongly, as it turns out – that what's upcoming is a replica of their live show. 'Run Run Run' is one of the better songs, bashed out with a driving Stones-like enthusiasm but it's a tad monotonous and not one of Pete's better compositions. There's whining feedback in the guitar solo which is ahead of its time, but as an opener it's a disappointment. This song was a first recorded by a band called The Cat on the Reaction label, which Pete produced.

BORIS THE SPIDER
(Entwistle)

The first ever John Entwistle song to appear on a Who album sets the pattern for the kind of off-beat macabre material for which John would become notorious as the years went by. Having been ordered by Pete to write two songs, John did very little until the eve of the session when Pete asked him how he was getting

on. No problem, he replied. How does it go, asked Pete. Like this, said John, humming the first few bars that came into his head. 'Boris' was the result.

Slightly discordant, as many of John's songs would be, 'Boris' has an abruptly descending chorus line and a sort of middle eight with the words 'Creepy crawly' repeated many times in the kind of off-key falsetto voice that parents use to frighten young children. With John dropping to a *basso profundo* for the hook line, it proved a stage favourite and was the only song on the whole album to endure throughout The Who's live career, offering light relief in concerts crammed with Pete's weightier songs. Justifiably proud of this composition, John would wear his spider emblem around his neck at almost every Who performance.

I NEED YOU
(Moon)

Daft lyrics aside, Keith's vocal contribution to the album takes its harmonies directly from The Beatles and although it's about as lightweight as The Who ever got in their early days, Keith managed to inject a certain wistful poignancy into his earliest known composition. There's also some thunderous drumming and a mock country and western harpsichord solo played by the ever present Nicky Hopkins.

WHISKEY MAN
(Entwistle)

John's second 'Quick One' contribution, about an inveterate boozer, lacks the punch of 'Boris', and the wit, but retains the slightly slurred vocal – appropriate on this title – and slightly off-key pitching, perhaps brought on by the DT's in this case, that became characteristic of John's writing and singing style.

HEATWAVE
(Holland, Dozier, Holland)

The Who's ability to turn R&B into rock was unique at the time and their stab at Martha And The Vandella's hit is probably the closest they ever came to capturing their 'Maximum R&B' style on record. This is tight and lively but a bit short, and

is one of two versions of the song the group recorded. The other can be found on 'Two's Missing' (see below).

COBWEBS AND STRANGE
(Moon)

Keith's second composition was an eccentric instrumental outing, featuring drums and a brass band of sorts, all clanging together to what sounds remarkably like a children's nursery rhyme theme. Slight but charming and typically Moon, who conveyed the melody to the rest of the band by whistling it.

By all accounts the scene in the studio when this was recorded was as eccentric as the track itself, with Kit Lambert leading the band in circles while they played assorted brass and percussion instruments: Pete on bass drum, Roger on trombone, Keith on tuba and John – according to Townshend the only one really playing anything – on trumpet.

DON'T LOOK AWAY

Lightweight country and western style pop with pleasant enough vocal harmonies, but a weak, unconvincing guitar solo suggests that this was a throwaway song by Pete. The melody is not unlike one of the themes from 'A Quick One' which suggests he did a quick re-write to fill up the album, either on this outing or on the mini-opera to come.

SEE MY WAY
(Daltrey)

The first of only two solo compositional credits by Roger in the entire Who catalogue sounds like a pastiche of something Buddy Holly might have written early in his career, then rejected. It was never recorded by The Who as a band; instead it's just Roger and Pete making a demo at Pete's home studio, then in London's Soho. Keith's drums are needed to fill out the sound.

Roger: "Nothing would please me more than to be able to write songs, but unfortunately I'm not a songwriter. Believe me, if anybody's tried, I have. I'm not a natural."

SO SAD ABOUT US

The best song on the album, written originally as a power pop effort for The Merseybeats, The Who's version is a feast of ringing power chords and harmony vocals fired off at a terrific pace over one of Pete's catchiest early melodies, with the whole band on top form. Listen out for the lovely counterpoint guitar lines that thread their way into the chorus, and the staccato guitar solo around the basic melody riff. Of all the lyricists working at the time, only Townshend had no qualms about slipping in la-la-las without compunction. 'So Sad...' is full of them, and all the better for it, but it also features the great line: 'But you can't switch off my loving like you can't switch off the sun'.

A QUICK ONE WHILE HE'S AWAY

Pete's first attempt at a rock opera was inspired, original, mildly amusing but rather clumsy and, apart from its rousing climax, a bit of a plodder on stage. It would never have been written had the other members' own compositions not come up short, so Kit Lambert proposed as a solution that Pete write a mini-opera to fill up ten minutes at the end of Side two. 'A Quick One' was certainly complex, moving through six specific sections, all with different melodies of their own, ranging from camp country and western to lush harmonies and all out power pop, with a touch of English music hall in between. There is also a rousing Who-like power chord climax with quite stunning vocal harmonies, especially John's falsetto.

The six songs are 'Her Man's Gone', 'Crying Town', 'We Have A Remedy', 'Ivor The Engine Driver', 'Soon Be Home' and 'You Are Forgiven'. Along the way the unnamed heroine pines for her absent lover, chooses Ivor as a substitute, regrets her folly when her man returns, confesses her indiscretion and is ultimately forgiven.

'A Quick One' has its flaws but it was ambitious, especially for its time, and pointed the way towards a future for The Who.

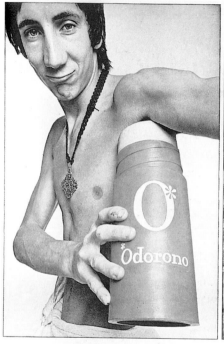

THE WHO SELL OUT

THE WHO SELL OUT

Replacing the stale smell of excess with the sweet smell of success, Peter Townshend, who, like nine out of ten stars, needs it. Face the music with "Odorono," the all-day deodorant that turns perspiration into inspiration.

This way to a cowboy's breakfast. Daltrey rides again. Thinks: "Thanks to Heinz Baked Beans everyday is a super day." Those who know how many beans make five get Heinz beans inside and outside at every opportunity. Get saucy.

THE WHO SELL OUT

ORIGINAL UK ISSUE: TRACK 612 002 (MONO) & TRACK 613 002 (STEREO), RELEASED NOVEMBER 1967; UK CD: POLYDOR 835 727-24. US: DECCA DL 4950 (MONO), DL 74950 (STEREO), CD: MCAD 31332.

Sometime between 1967 and 1968 The Who ceased to be a pop group any longer and became, arguably, Britain's first ever *rock band*. It was a transition that few of their contemporaries were able to make, and the two likeliest contenders – The Beatles and The Rolling Stones – had problems making the shift which The Who didn't have. The Beatles' enormous popularity meant that they were unable to perform live any longer – and muscular live performance was a pre-requisite of being a *rock band* – while the Stones were grounded through drug busts and Brian Jones' inability to cut it on stage. The Who, erstwhile bronze medallists behind The Beatles and the Stones in the Sixties Pop Olympiad, thus shot through the gap and for a brief shining moment – three years actually – became the greatest of Britain's rock bands, and certainly the best live act in the world.

They and Cream (who unlike The Who were formed for the purpose) pioneered the modern concept of rock performance and touring, ushering in an era which lasts in far more sophisticated forms to this day. After The Who's tours of this period, no longer would groups perform their hits in 20 minute sets and then retire. From now on they would be expected to perform for at least an hour and generally longer, and offer music from their LPs, performed loudly and in a manner that enhanced the original recordings, either through sheer volume or musical virtuosity or both. They would also be expected to improvise, to offer some form of liberating stage show and even to perform unrecorded material hitherto unheard by many in the audience.

All of this occurred following the release of The Who's first pop-art masterpiece concept LP. Largely overlooked at the time but now a reference point for so many pilgrims, The Who, and Pete in particular, embrace outside influences like acid rock and surrealism with a pop sensibility that gives the songs a far surer touch than those on the previous album. Nevertheless, they never sound like anyone else, partly because Keith had by now confirmed his position as the most expressive drummer in rock and John the most fluid bass guitarist, but mainly because of Pete's songwriting style and the way in which he and Roger, and occasionally John, sang harmony vocals together. The Who had a definite style of their own which might have been influenced by others but which others were never able to copy.

The songs on the first side of 'The Who Sell Out' are linked together by spoof commercials similar to those heard on pirate radio stations, and in many ways the album stands as a tribute to the pirates who plugged their singles and did so much to help The Who's career. Why this idea wasn't carried over to the second side is any-body's guess, especially as further recorded commercials which could have appeared on Side two have since come to light. The sleeve design also enforced the 'Sell Out' concept, with the members of the group 'promoting' a variety of commercial products: Roger sits in a tub of baked beans (apparently he nearly caught pneumonia sitting in the cold tub during the shoot), Pete uses an underarm deodorant, Keith applies spot cream, and John extols the virtues of a body building course.

For all its imagination 'The Who Sell Out' reached only a disappointing number 13 in the UK LP charts, and failed completely in the US despite the heavy touring schedule that the band were undertaking over there. Because of the touring, it was recorded variously in London, New York and Los Angeles, and there were even some unpro-ductive sessions in Nashville.

ARMENIA CITY IN THE SKY
(Speedy Keene)

Affable Speedy Keene was first the drummer and then guitarist and occasional songwriter for Thunderclap Newman, the band for whom Pete produced the number one hit single 'Something In The Air' in 1969. Before that he hung around Track Records, hoping for work. This song, space-age grunge thirty years ahead of its time with Roger at the top of his vocal range, is dense, acid-tinged rock with a guitar solo enhanced by electronic whooping effects, backwards tapes and a thick organ sound quite unlike anything else on the album. Most fans probably thought 'Armenia' was written by Pete anyway, so close is the style to his own writing.

HEINZ BAKED BEANS

The first of several spoof commercials on 'Sell Out' is devoted to the traditional English tea time dish beloved of kids. Actually it's a re-write of 'Cobwebs And Strange' from the second album with added vocals.

MARY ANNE WITH THE SHAKY HAND(S)

Pete's second great song about masturbation – the first was 'Pictures Of Lily' – or a tasteless ode to an afflicted unfortunate? Either way 'Mary Anne' is one of the stand-out tracks on 'Sell Out' that could have been a single had Pete not been in the midst of writing a series of even better songs for singles, most of which didn't appear on albums at the time. There was also the question of good taste, or at least what the self-appointed arbiters of good taste might feel about the song's subject matter.

'Mary Anne' opens with lovely acoustic chords which get better as Roger attempts to explain why the heroine is preferable to Jean, Cindy and the other girls on the block. Again there's a lovely chorded solo with Pete stretching out the notes on his acoustic guitar.

Once again The Who are well ahead of the pack when it comes to subject material, but whatever the lyrics, 'Mary Anne' would have been a winner on the melody alone. An alternative and quite different take on 'Mary', featuring electric guitar instead of acoustic, appeared in the US as the B-side of their 'I Can See For Miles' single, and in the US 'Hand' became 'Hands'. This also featured Roger singing the word 'S-h-a-k-y' through a tremolo effect to give a truly shaky feel!

ODORONO

The second spoof advert, this time an extended ditty extolling the virtues of a deodorant. 'Mr Davidson', incidentally, is probably Harold Davidson, a well known London booking agent of the time. The mono take is very different from the stereo take.

TATTOO

A string of lovely arpeggios opens one of Pete's finest 'rites of passage' songs, based around the idea that tattoos make 'a man a man'. 'Tattoo' is another stand-out track from 'Sell Out' and one for which The Who retained an affection long after all the other songs – barring 'I Can

See For Miles' – had become passé. They were performing it live right up to the mid-Seventies.

'Tattoo' boasts a particularly attractive and mature melody, and couplets with unusually complex rhymes about two brothers who decide to get them-selves tattooed, only to regret the decision after parental objections and personal contemplation.

OUR LOVE WAS (IS)

Pure pop with the kind of cascading ethereal harmonies at which The Who were by now becoming most adept, space age guitar work and an unusual chorus which works up to a final upward key change. Another potential single had not Pete already had enough singles in his pocket to keep fans happy for years. Again, the mono version is a completely different mix from the stereo version, notably Pete's guitar track.

In the US this song was entitled 'Our Love Was, Is'.

I CAN SEE FOR MILES

Many fans' choice as the best Who single ever, preceded here by their price-less advert for Rotosound strings (as used by JE): "Hold your group together... with Rotosound Strings".

The Who never sounded more together than on this superbly crafted long-distance single. Psychedelic without being trippy, it strains at the leash but is held together by Pete's taut, sustained guitar phrases, Keith's immaculate drum-ming, particularly under the melody, and a crackling electric feel. The solo is revela-tion: buzzing feedback, choppy chords and Keith at his very best. Pete's two overdubbed guitar parts could never be replicated in concert which is why The Who rarely performed this all-time favourite on stage until 1989 when Steve Bolton joined the on-stage band.

The failure of 'I Can See For Miles' to become a significant hit single (it reached number 10 in the UK, and number 9 in the US) was a profound disappointment for Pete.

"To me that was the ultimate Who record yet it didn't sell," said Pete at the time. "I spat on the British record buyer."

The fact that 'The Last Waltz', a saccha-rine waltz of appaling sentimentality by the wretched Engelbert Humperdinck, was on top at the time can't have helped.

CAN'T REACH YOU

Another great pop rock song, this time with Pete on vocals, with flowing harmonies and a lovely chorus, slightly marred by Pete's uninspired guitar solo, but a fine example of The Who's mid-Sixties style. This one was originally conceived as an 'aircrash' song in which a survivor was unable to reach a dying loved one.

MEDAC
(Entwistle)

John's light-hearted, Gilbert and Sullivanesque spoof commercial for spot cream.

RELAX

Acid rock *à la* early Pink Floyd, not The

Who's natural territory, especially as the song is organ based, but the dense sound they achieve soars to great heights of psychedelia during the central instrumental passage. Pete Townshend was no stranger to the UFO Club in London's Tottenham Court Road where the Syd Barrett led Pink Floyd were regulars on the cramped stage; indeed, Pete's future wife Karen Astley designed UFO posters at the time.

SILAS STINGY
(Entwistle)

An attractive but still sinister little pop ditty about a miser sung more tunefully than most Entwistle pieces and featuring a novel churchlike organ in the background. This is appropriate for its precisely arranged choral exchanges. Veers towards a novelty, but Abba certainly borrowed the 'Money, Money, Money' line in their song of the same name.

SUNRISE

Virtually a Townshend solo piece, the first of many that would appear throughout The

Who's catalogue, 'Sunrise' finds Pete in romantic mood, picking on an acoustic guitar and singing a beautiful, high-pitched melody well beyond Roger's range.

Pete: "This one utilises quite a lot of chords picked up from Micky Baker's 'Jazz Guitar' tutors. They come in two parts, show all complex chords as box diagrams and will teach you more in an hour about jazz guitar than you will ever learn elsewhere."

RAEL

The chord progression in the second half of 'Rael' is best known for its more carefully balanced appearance as a central theme of 'Tommy', where it becomes the instrumental passage in both 'Sparks' and the longer 'Underture'. On its first outing here, it forms the climax to Pete's second mini-opera, a more melodic, compact and altogether more balanced affair than 'A Quick One'. Although no narrative is evident from the lyrics, 'Rael' has a slightly ethereal, unearthly feel and its musical components – including some lovely high harmony singing – slot

together in the same manner that Pete adopted in 'Tommy', albeit with far greater complexity. Here, the famous 'Tommy' riff is emphasised by a deep, echoey, crashing sound, rather like the amplified noise of snooker balls smashing into one another but more likely to be Pete experimenting with the reverb control on his amp.

It's been suggested that 'Rael' is an abbreviation for Israel, that the 'Red Chins' referred to are Red Chinese and that the song is politically motivated. Either way 'Rael' is definitely a place, as the coda ('Rael 2') released on The Who's 4-CD box set (see below), makes clear. Pete has written that a portion of the plot concerned the Chinese crushing established religions as their expanding population eventually takes over the whole world. But interpretations are meaningless as Pete himself admitted. "No-one will ever know what it means," he said. "It has been squeezed up too tightly to make sense."

TOMMY

ORIGINAL UK ISSUE TRACK 613013/4; RELEASED MAY 1969: UK CD: POLYDOR 800 077-2. US: DECCA DXSW 7205; CD: MCAD 10005 (2 DISCS), MCAD 10801 (1 DISC); GOLD: MCA UDCD533 (1 DISC).

The Who made 'Tommy' and 'Tommy' made The Who. That's the popular conception of the 'rock opera' that turned them into superstars and millionaires within the space of 12 months. There is no doubt that 'Tommy' rescued The Who from financial ruin, but it proved also to be a weight around their necks which lingers on to this day; at the time of writing, as a Broadway-style stage musical set to tour the globe. Although 'Quadrophenia' was a more complex work on which the writing, playing, singing and production was superior in every way, it is 'Tommy' for which The Who will be remembered above all else, save perhaps for the song 'My Generation'.

Recorded with Kit Lambert waving the baton back at London's IBC Studios during the early months on 1969, 'Tommy' brought together all of Pete's influences and aspirations in one great rag-bag of ideas and ideals: he's a Messiah figure elevated despite enormous disabilities to an other-worldly loftiness, brought down by reality and, finally, turned into a rock superstar-style deity. That's one view, the one that explains why Meher Baba, the Indian spiritual figure to whom Pete had lately become attracted, is credited as avatar. The other view is that 'Tommy' is simply great rock music, almost 90 minutes worth, in which the form is explored every which way with extraordinary precision and timing and thus becomes a text book on riffing, rock harmonics, interlocking rhythms, electric and acoustic guitar backing, bass fluidity, vocal harmonies and every other skill with which a premier league rock band ought to be equipped.

There is an almost mathematical precision to 'Tommy' in the way that musical motifs – the 'Pinball' intro, the 'See Me Feel Me' chorus, the 'Underture'/'Sparks' melody, the 'Go To The Mirror' riff – are introduced in the overture, then repeated at various moments throughout. Because these motifs crop up repeatedly in this manner, 'Tommy' becomes much easier to assimilate on first listening than a double album of non-interconnected songs.

Pete and his friend Richard Barnes produced a whole book on 'Tommy' in an attempt to explain it all, and on stage Tommy took on a whole other dimension – that's where it *really* became great – but it's the record we're concerned with here. The original album, opulently packaged in a beautifully designed, surreal, triple-gatefold sleeve complete with libretto, was – by current standards – poorly produced in the studio and sounds very flat compared to certain other records in The Who's catalogue. The more recent MCA Records single CD version on which every song has been remastered is an improvement but it's still not perfect. But buy this instead of the Polydor double CD which has poor hi-fi and actually costs more.

Despite the perfect timing – its mystical themes were ideal for 1969 – and general hullabaloo surrounding its release, 'Tommy' stalled at number 2 in the UK charts and at number 4 in the US, but in America it stayed on the charts for 47 weeks, far longer than any other Who album. A 'Gold' remastered CD (which contains a different vocal track on 'Eyesight To The Blind') is available in the US.

OVERTURE

A proper opera needs a proper overture and like all overtures this one contains a well arranged mixed bag of instrumental versions of snatches of the songs that will follow, most of them linked together by the rumbling, bass-heavy 'Go To The Mirror' riff. The guitar parts are played on Pete's acoustic Gibson J200, which sets a mood for the entire work, but John's French horn adds interesting melodic touches and, as ever, the choral work and drums are quite superb. The best moment in the overture comes towards the end when an organ arrives to pound out the 'Listening To You' melody from the 'See Me Feel Me' excerpt. At the close Pete is left strumming alone for a segue into...

IT'S A BOY

... Tommy's birth, a brief introductory piece sung in a high register by Pete, followed by some impressive acoustic guitar work, leading into...

1921 (YOU DIDN'T HEAR IT)

... the first melodic track, this one sung by Pete who wrote several beautiful ballads for 'Tommy'. This is one of them, although the song itself is intercut with a harsher refrain in which Tommy's stepdad urges his mistress's newly born son to forget anything he's ever seen or heard... with disastrous consequences. Without this section, '1921' could have become a hit for anyone. In the US '1921' was titled 'You Didn't Hear It'.

AMAZING JOURNEY

The first great rock song on the album and a song which was a cornerstone for the whole 'Tommy' project contrasts Keith's 'lead-the-way' drums with the lighter timbre that Roger adopted for most of 'Tommy'. With backwards tapes to emphasise the state of Tommy's unbalanced mind, 'Amazing Journey' is one of many 'Tommy' songs that came to life on stage and it segues directly into...

SPARKS

... the first instrumental track, a deep-rooted, rumbling riff, endlessly repeated until, coming up for air, it slides into the better known 'Rael' melody that is explored at greater depth in 'Underture'.

EYESIGHT FOR THE BLIND (THE HAWKER)

(Sonny Boy Williamson)

The only non-original song on 'Tommy' is this brief excursion into a piece by Sonny

Boy Williamson which is referred to as 'The Hawker' in the libretto. The heaviest number so far, it includes several references to Tommy's handicaps, thus helping to further the plot and sounding for all the world as if Pete wrote it himself. There's a different vocal on the 'Gold' disc.

CHRISTMAS

'Christmas', with its nagging, slightly off-key background vocal, is the first really Who-like song on 'Tommy', upbeat and slightly unnerving. At its heart is the first reference to the 'See Me Feel Me' motif, 'Tommy's' most dramatic theme.

COUSIN KEVIN
(Entwistle)

John's first 'Tommy' song suits his off-beat, macabre style, telling the tale of Tommy's encounter with his cousin Kevin, the school bully, who does unspeakable things to the unfortunate boy. John's vocal is in a very high key and a sitar can be heard deep in the mix.

THE ACID QUEEN

Certainly one of the best songs on 'Tommy', 'The Acid Queen' features Pete on vocals for what appears to be an overtly drug oriented song with strong rock melodies and an infectious hook, but there's more to it than meets the eye...

Pete: "The song's not just about acid; it's the whole drug thing, the drink thing, the sex thing wrapped into one big ball. It's about how you get it laid on you that if you haven't fucked forty birds, taken sixty trips, drunk fourteen pints or whatever... society – people – force it on you. She represents this force."

UNDERTURE

A very lengthy instrumental version of the melody from 'Rael' on 'The Who Sell Out', played on acoustic guitar in its entirety, with Keith's pounding drums hustling it along. On stage 'Underture'/'Sparks'/'Rael' (version) – whatever you care to name it – became a *pièce de résistance* of ensemble Who playing, with the band reaching higher and higher towards those block chord climaxes that defined their style. Here, they adopt a far lighter approach.

DO YOU THINK IT'S ALRIGHT

A quick vocal link into...

FIDDLE ABOUT
(Entwistle)

... which tells of Tommy's dreadful experiences at the hands of the family pervert and was an ideal vehicle for John's warped sense of humour. The wicked Uncle Ernie, presumably Kevin's dad, would eventually become synonymous with Keith's more depraved caricatures. Here it's a mildly amusing comic song which, like 'Cousin Kevin', John's other contribution to 'Tommy', sounds a bit out of place among Pete's songs. John sang this live when 'Tommy' was first aired on stage in its entirety but Keith took over later and revelled in its malevolence.

PINBALL WIZARD

Pete Townshend has often been called the greatest rhythm guitarist in rock, and no better evidence survives than the furious acoustic strumming which underpins 'Pinball Wizard', the best known song from 'Tommy' and a serious contender for the best Who song of all time.

From the opening minor chords to the upward key change near the end, 'Pinball' is a rock *tour de force*, brimful of ideas, power chords, great lyrics and ensemble playing as tight as anything anywhere. The concept of a deaf, dumb and blind pinball champion might stretch the imagination but anything can be forgiven in the context of this song.

The idea of a pinball Messiah came from Nik Cohn, the UK's hottest rock writer in the Sixties and a personal friend of Pete and Kit Lambert, whose girlfriend at the time really was a pinball queen. At the time Cohn was writing rock reviews for the *New York Times* and there seems little doubt that he was strong-armed into giving 'Tommy' a rave review on the strength of its pinball connection.

Be that as it may, nothing takes away the sheer delight of this number, one of only two (the other was 'See Me Feel

Me') from 'Tommy' to outlast the rest of the opera and remain in The Who's live set for as long as they appeared on stage.

As a single, which was slightly speeded up from the album version, 'Pinball' reached number 4 in the UK charts and number 19 in the US. Elton John sang it in the 'Tommy' movie and his version reached number 7 in the UK. Curiously, it was also covered by The New Seekers (in a medley with 'See Me Feel Me'), whose version reached number 16.

THERE'S A DOCTOR

A quick link into...

GO TO THE MIRROR

... another key 'Tommy' song – he discovers he can see his reflection, a leap forward in the healing process – which seamlessly juxtaposes a second refrain of 'See Me Feel Me' with the 'Listening To You' coda into the heavier 'Mirror' riff.

TOMMY CAN YOU HEAR ME

Roger leads The Who in a folksy sing-along in virtual unison, accompanied only

by Pete's ringing acoustic guitar and John's springy bass; lightweight but catchy.

SMASH THE MIRROR

A brief, dramatic snatch highlighted by the ascending 'Rise, rise rise' lyrics and the sound of breaking glass.

SENSATION

'Sensation' was written long before 'Tommy' was formulated, apparently about a girl Pete met during The Who's disastrous tour of Australia in 1968. Nevertheless, its lyrics are appropriate, as is the catchy, lightweight pop rhythm. Pete sings lead vocals.

MIRACLE CURE

A newspaper vendor offers a quick link into...

SALLY SIMPSON

The subject matter of 'Sally Simpson' may well have been one of the key elements that inspired Pete to produce 'Tommy' in the first place, but it sounds as if it belongs on another album entirely. Missing are the rhythmic structures that crop up so often elsewhere, to be replaced by a rather slight melody as befits a narrative song about how Sally disobeys her parents, heads out to see 'Tommy' in concert, gets caught up in a crush in front of the stage and is permanently disfigured as a result.

The song was inspired by an incident that occurred when The Who played with The Doors at the Singer Bowl in New York. Pete apparently saw the way Jim Morrison was teasing the front row, and the dangerous situation he created.

I'M FREE

A memorable six chord riff introduces one of the best 'Tommy' songs in which he throws off the shackles of his handicaps, and urges his followers – those attracted by his prowess at 'Pinball' – to follow him. Tinkly piano, a great acoustic solo and nice re-use of the familiar 'Pinball' intro riff.

WELCOME

The gentlest song on the album with Roger at his most melodic speeds up in the middle, with Roger on harmonica, then returns to its mannered, rather dreamy aura.

TOMMY'S HOLIDAY CAMP
(Moon)

Keith's sole writing credit on 'Tommy' is one minute of Pete's vocal over a fairground barrel organ extolling the virtues of the holiday camp which Tommy has established as a base for his mission.

WE'RE NOT GONNA TAKE IT (SEE ME FEEL ME)

Two songs in one, the first a catchy riff based piece about rejecting fascism and the second a circular, looping prayer for unification. With its churning major chords, the finale to 'Tommy' is among the most simple yet effective pieces of music that Pete Townshend has ever written. 'See Me, Feel Me' is the most obvious hymn to Baba – or any deity – in

The Who's catalogue, although there are other less obvious examples in the 'Lifehouse' cycle of songs and in 'Quadrophenia'. 'Listening to you...' is crystal clear homage and when it was played live it appeared for all the world as if The Who were paying a remarkable tribute to the audience they were singing to. In this respect, it couldn't fail to lift the spirits – just as all hymns are designed to do. And when the bright lights were switched on, The Who's auditoria became giant cathedrals in which, briefly, preachers and congregation were united in a massed celebration of rock music as the force for unification that Pete Townshend truly believed it was meant to be. Hell, disabled fans even waved their crutches in the air; maybe one or two even walked out of the show without them.

LIVE AT LEEDS

ORIGINAL UK ISSUE: TRACK 2406 001, RELEASED MAY 1970; UK CD: POLYDOR 825 339-2.
US DECCA DL 79175; CD: MCAD 37000.

'Live At Leeds' was the best live rock album of its era, and was designed to spotlight the other, non-'Tommy', side of The Who, the rough and ready in-yer-face rock band that they'd always been before conceptual artistry side-tracked their principal writer. "Some people think the band's called Tommy and the album's called The Who," muttered Entwistle. 'Live At Leeds' put a stop to that.

Its packaging was an antidote to 'Tommy' too: a plain buff sleeve, roughly rubber stamped with the band's name and looking for all the world like a bootleg. Within could be found an envelope containing all sorts of facsimile Who ephemera (photos, date sheets, contracts, lyrics) and a record on which there was a handwritten warning that the crackles were not the fault of your record player.

To watch The Who live at the tail end of the Sixties on a good night was to experience the very best that live rock could offer, anywhere in the world. This album – and a few stray bits of video footage and as yet unreleased tapes – are all that remain as evidence to support the claim that The Who were the world's best when it came to performance. On this showing the claim is surely upheld.

At the time of writing there were plans to update 'Live At Leeds' by including an extra 30 minutes' worth of material from the same concert in order to bring the CD running

time up to around 70 minutes, and to include a small booklet with an essay on the band and photographs taken at Leeds University on the night in question, February 14, 1970.

For the record, the complete Who set that night ran as follows: Heaven And Hell, I Can't Explain, Fortune Teller, Tattoo, Young Man Blues, Substitute, Happy Jack, I'm A Boy, A Quick One, Tommy (Overture, It's A Boy, 1921, Amazing Journey, Sparks, Eyesight To The Blind, Christmas, Acid Queen, Pinball Wizard, Fiddle About, Tommy Can You Hear Me, There's A Doctor, Go To The Mirror, Miracle Cure/Sally Simpson, I'm Free, Tommy's Holiday Camp, We're Not Gonna Take It/See Me Feel Me), Summertime Blues, Shaking All Over, My Generation, Magic Bus.

'Live At Leeds' reached number 3 in the UK album charts and number 4 in the US.

YOUNG MAN BLUES
(Mose Allison)

Mose Allison's blues song, which he first recorded in 1957, is given a whole new lease of life in The Who's violent stop-start reading. Its attack and counter attack, with Keith leading the assault against Roger's vocals, John contributing his usual high speed runs and Pete slashing away on a blues riff until the solo allows him to stretch out. The version here is tighter and more assured than usual, not quite as long as they sometimes played it but hugely impressive as a showcase for The Who's wayward streams.

SUBSTITUTE

Townshend's first comment on illusion... he always said The Who were a substitute for The Rolling Stones. This short, sharp, snappy 'Substitute' is as tight a performance as any live version around, although it lacks the punchy solo and false ending of the single. (See also 'Meaty Beaty Big And Bouncy'.)

SUMMERTIME BLUES
(Cochran/Capehart)

Eddie Cochran's bouncy, rhythmic guitar style influenced Pete enormously in The Who's early days and their version of 'Summertime Blues' was a highlight of the band's stage shows for many years. Pete's block chord slash style, coupled with John's rumbling bass riff, was ideal for this song of teenage angst, and Roger, eternally a rocker at heart, loved to sing it. John always supplied the bass vocal line with a wry smile. Cochran died in 1960 and by 1968 The Who had made 'Summertime Blues' their very own, but there's no question that Eddie would have been proud that his best known song had become a staple in the

set list of a live act as great as The Who. Also released as a single in an edited version in 1970.

Other Cochran songs essayed by The Who included 'C'Mon Everybody' and the lesser known 'My Way'.

SHAKING ALL OVER
(Fred Heath aka Johnny Kidd)

With the possible exception of 'Move It', 'Dynamite' and 'It'll Be Me' – the only decent records Cliff Richard has ever released – 'Shaking All Over' is the only pre-Beatles UK rock'n'roll song of any serious merit, and also the best. With its startling guitar riff, heavy bass line, minor key and lyrics that really do shake and rock, 'Shakin' All Over' sounds exactly like it could have been written by one of the great American Fifties rock songwriters, maybe even Eddie Cochran or Leiber & Stoller. Instead it was written by the leader of The Pirates, one of the first truly ballsy rock'n'roll bands in Britain. Contemporaries of The Detours (as The Who were then known), it was The Pirates, with their singer, guitar, bass and

drums line-up, who convinced Roger Daltrey that he should abandon his own guitar, fire The Detours' singer and occupy centre stage himself. That left Pete as their sole guitarist and he took no little notice of Pirates' guitarist Mick Green whenever the two bands shared a bill, which was often.

The Who's 'Shakin' All Over' is a typical full frontal assault, guaranteed to rouse anyone within earshot. Everyone gets a chance to shine, especially Roger who loves singing a good rocker. In concert The Who speeded up in the middle and occasionally segued into Willie Dixon's 'Spoonful' and then back again into 'Shakin'' for the finale. In fact, they did this at Leeds as the unedited tapes (and bootleg albums) reveal.

MY GENERATION

'My Generation' went through many transformations whenever The Who played it live. Often it became a slow blues that gradually speeded up but here, on what must be one of the longest versions of the song that The Who ever performed, it starts traditionally before meandering off after the bass solo into sections from 'Tommy', including a whipped-up verse of 'See Me Feel Me', some unsecured blues and R&B hollering, and some excellent soloing by Pete who appears to play against his own echo bouncing off the back of the hall. There are many false endings and Pete often silences the band before heading off into uncharted territory, apparently finishing the song on several occasions, only to restart and accelerate again.

This version of 'My Generation' is as good an example as any of the way in which The Who could play off each other when they were in the mood. By now, barring Keith, they'd been playing together on stage for around eight years, and there's no substitute for intuition built on such experience. Listen for Keith's repeated sixth-sense count-ins, all pre-empted by a Pete line that's familiar only to him and John, and – as ever – listen to John working overtime as he zooms up and down the longest bass fretboard in rock.

For sheer undiluted Who at their absolute live best, this track, all 14 minutes of it, takes some beating.

MAGIC BUS

With its Bo Diddley beat and room for stretching out on guitar, Pete loved to play 'Magic Bus' but John, anchored to a 'dub du-du du-du-dub, dub dub' riff on 'A', hated it. There wasn't much opportunity for Keith either, but he always looked pleased as punch to be making silly faces and tapping away on his little wooden block while Pete and Roger swapped those preposterous lines about trading the magic bus in for 'two hundred English pounds'.

As a single 'Magic Bus' was a minor hit in 1968. As a stage number, it became a crowd favourite if for no other reason than it was quite unlike anything else The Who ever performed. Like everything else on 'Leeds' bar 'Substitute', the version here is extended well beyond its normal running time. It's also a great showcase for Pete and Roger is no slouch on harmonica.

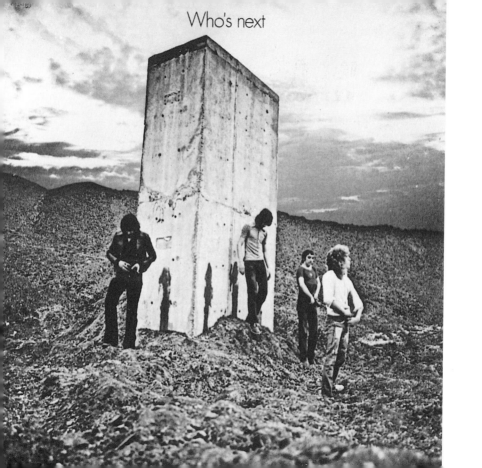
Who's next

WHO'S NEXT

ORIGINAL UK ISSUE: TRACK 2408 102, RELEASED JULY 1971; UK CD: POLYDOR 813651;
US: DECCA 79182; CD: MCAD 37217.

'Who's Next' is widely regarded as the finest studio LP The Who ever recorded and one of the best rock records ever. Certainly, it's far and away their most consistent in terms of quality songs – there isn't a duffer among them – and it introduces an important new element, the synthesizer, into the group's overall sound. More importantly, The Who were now at their creative peak, both as individual musicians and as a band: on stage they regularly performed with breathtaking panache, their confidence was at an all time high, and their status as one of the world's great rock bands was secured for eternity.

'Who's Next' started life as another of Pete's concepts, this one a movie/musical called 'Lifehouse' which contained enough songs for a double LP, but the project became bogged down in its futuristic, philosophical complexities and was eventually reduced to a single LP and no movie. The concept of 'Lifehouse' is long and bewildering, and the random nature of the songs on 'Who's Next' gives little clue as to its story line, such as it was. In view of what 'Who's Next' became, there is little point in trying to explain it here, but among its many ideals was Pete's design for The Who to somehow become one with their audience, to break down totally the barrier that exists between audience and performer. U2 have been grappling with a similar ideal throughout their career.

What makes 'Who's Next' different from any of its predecessors is the clarity of sound afforded by producer Glyn Johns, who took over from Kit Lambert midway through this project. Lambert was the perfect foil for Pete to bounce ideas off and his creative influence on The Who cannot be over-emphasised, but he was no technician, and as hi-fi equipment and recording studios became more and more sophisticated during the Seventies, far greater attention was being paid to the way records actually sounded. The second great leap forward on 'Who's Next' was Pete's introduction of synthesizers into The Who's sound, most notably on 'Baba O'Riley' and 'Won't Get Fooled Again', the two songs that open and close this album. Unlike so many of his less imaginative peers Pete didn't use his synthesizer simply as a solo keyboard that could make funny noises, but as a rotating musical loop which underpinned the melody and added a sharp bite to the rhythm track. In this respect, he (and Stevie Wonder) were the first musicians of their generation to make proper creative use of this new and much abused electronic toy. Townshend's synthesizer style on 'Who's Next', in fact, is the first appearance on a rock record of the repetitive electronic sequencing that is so predominant on Nineties pop and dance music.

There were other leaps forward here, too. Pete's songwriting showed a sustained level of brilliance he would never again achieve (although he came close on 'Quadrophenia'), John's bass lines were more melodic but as fluid as ever, and Keith managed to rein in his wilder antics while maintaining his usual key expressive role. But perhaps the greatest musical triumph was Roger's: the 'Tommy' experience had improved his confidence as a vocalist immeasurably and it shows, whether on the melodies of the beautiful 'Behind Blue Eyes' and 'Song Is Over' or, at the other extreme, the torturous scream that climaxes 'Won't Get Fooled Again'.

Most of the songs that appeared on 'Who's Next', together with other 'Lifehouse' material that later appeared on singles and on 'Odds And Sods' (see below), were originally recorded in New York with Kit Lambert as producer, but the band weren't satisfied with the results and returned to London to re-record them at Olympic Studios

in Barnes with Glyn Johns. This is why bootlegs which have appeared on the market offer interesting alternative versions of many of the songs (that feature Leslie West on lead guitar and Al Kooper on organ). Full details of the whole 'Lifehouse' story and the making of the album can be found in a fascinating unpublished manuscript entitled *The Who: Lifehouse and The Making of Who's Next* by John Atkins, co-editor of *Generations* magazine.

'Who's Next' became the only Who album to make number one in the UK charts. It peaked at number four in the US, but songs from the album are played continually on US radio stations to this day. Long terms plans for a repackaged CD will bring the running time up to around 70 minutes with the inclusion of other tracks Pete wrote for 'Lifehouse'.

BABA O'RILEY

Thirty seconds of spiralling solo synthesizer, excessively long for any intro, opens the album and one of its most memorable tracks. 'Baba', of course, is Meher Baba, Pete's spiritual pal, and O'Riley, is Terry Riley, the electronic composer whose work 'A Rainbow In Curved Air' inspired Pete's use of looping synthesizer riffs. Piano, voice, drums, bass and eventually guitar join in but it's the cut and thrust between Daltrey's leonine roar and Pete's tuneful pleading that gives the song its tension and best moments, though the free-form climax, a souped up Irish jig featuring Dave Arbus on violin and Keith playing as fast as he's ever played, is quite mesmerising.

'Teenage Wasteland', the starting point for Pete's imaginary generation in their search to find nirvana, became a timeless Who entity in Roger's hands, and the downright disgust at the way things have turned out (post-Woodstock) was never better expressed in rock.

Pete: "This was a number I wrote while I

was doing these experiments with tapes on the synthesizer. Among my plans was to take a person out of the audience and feed information – height, weight, autobiographical details – about the person into the synthesizer. The synthesizer would then select notes from the pattern of that person. It would be like translating a person into music. On this particular track I programmed details about the life of Meher Baba and that provided the backing for the number."

The synthesizer track that dominates 'Baba O'Riley' is part of a longer synthesizer piece that Pete released privately on his Meher Baba tribute LP 'I Am' in 1972. Further sections featured on his 'Psychoderelict' solo LP in 1993.

BARGAIN

Most songs addressed to 'you' are sentimental love songs but Pete's 'yous' are almost always addressed to Meher Baba, and, although used in songs that are often full-tilt rockers like the 'See Me Feel Me' climax to 'Tommy', they are actually not-so-cunningly disguised prayers soliciting forgiveness for his earthly foibles and unworthiness, seeking advice on spiritual advancement or simply offering thanks for his avatar's bountiful virtue. 'Bargain', which stands alongside any of the best tracks on 'Who's Next', is about the search for personal identity amid a sea of conformity, with lyrics such as 'I know I am nothing without you' giving the Baba slant away, especially when sung by Pete in a keening centre-piece counterpoint to Roger's harsher lines.

Although there's a low-key synthesizer track in the background, 'Bargain' shows off The Who's ensemble playing at its very best. Block chords abound, there's a terrific guitar solo, bass lines pop and crackle and Keith's drumming gives the song a rhythmic foundation that lifts The Who clean out of your speaker cabinets. A knock-out live version of 'Bargain' can be found on 'Who's Missing' (see below).

LOVE AIN'T FOR KEEPING
Seriously upfront acoustic guitars feature strongly throughout one of the slighter (and shortest) songs on 'Who's Next', but the bouncy tempo, relatively simple compared with other songs, and understated synthesizer hold this together well, as Roger sings about the difficulty of sustaining relationships in the modern world. This track is sequenced to run almost directly into...

MY WIFE
(Entwistle)
John's song of marital discontent is arguably the best he ever wrote for The Who and it provided them with a terrific stage rocker, complete with the kind of block chords that Pete loved to play while spinning his arm windmill-style. Although this version is no slouch, John was dissatisfied with the sound and re-recorded it himself on his third solo album. On live versions, Pete would stretch out the end, duelling with John to mesmerising effect. 'My Wife' is possibly the most 'Who-like' song John ever wrote, certainly the closest to Pete's style of writing, and the lyrics are quite hilarious.

SONG IS OVER

Among the most gorgeous ballads Pete has ever written, 'Song Is Over' again highlights the contrasting vocals of Roger and Pete, as well as some inspired synthesizer work, lovely piano playing by Nicky Hopkins, and a sumptuous production. Because of its complexity, it was never played live. Doubtless intended as the climax to 'Lifehouse', it features as a coda the motif from 'Pure And Easy' (see 'Odds And Sods' below), another key 'Lifehouse' song which was inexplicably left off the album. The closing passages are enhanced by an almost subliminal top-of-the-scale synthesizer harmonic line that traces the melody with a marvellous undulating counterpoint.

It is only by listening to this song, in conjunction with others like 'Pure And Easy', 'Baba O'Riley', 'Naked Eye', 'Time Is Passing' (which The Who never released) and 'Behind Blue Eyes' that the real potential of 'Lifehouse', at least from a purely musical point of view, can be truly appreciated. A rock opera, or at least a song cycle, based around material as strong as this would surely have been the rock masterpiece to end all rock masterpieces. When it failed to materialise in the way he envisaged, Pete's disillusion led to his first nervous breakdown and almost broke up the band.

GETTING IN TUNE

Using the time-honoured tradition of tuning up before a show as an allegory for creating harmony between disparate societies, 'Getting In Tune' is another fearless rocker, perhaps not quite so breathtaking as others from the album, but certainly no slouch. Like 'Song Is Over', a showcase for Roger at his absolute best.

GOING MOBILE

With its rolling, appropriately 'mobile' rhythm and absence of harsh chords, 'Going Mobile' lacks the grandeur of many of the other tracks on 'Who's Next', but it's a witty and worthy contender nevertheless, a 'travelogue' sung by Pete about the joys of driving around gypsy-style in his newly acquired holiday home. Lines about 'hippy gypsies' seem particularly apt in the current era of New Age travellers.

Apart from its tricky little acoustic rhythm signature, it's also notable for the guitar solo in which Pete wired his electric through a device similar to a wah-wah called an envelope follower, with the result that it sounds like he's playing underwater.

BEHIND BLUE EYES

Opening with one of the prettiest melodies Pete has ever written, 'Behind Blue Eyes' rightly became a Who classic almost immediately. Crystal clear acoustic guitar, Roger at his melodic best and a fluid bass line take the first verse, velvet three-part harmonies join in for the second, then, finally, in lurches Keith to give 'Blue Eyes' its third and final dimension.

The faster central passage, a plea to the creator for confidence and succour, contains the most moving lyrics on the whole album, before 'Blue Eyes' reverts back to its gentle opening lines at the close. The choirlike closing vocal harmony, drenched in reverb, is deliberately – and brilliantly – sequenced to contrast sharply with the shrill electronic synthesizer riff that heralds 'Won't Get Fooled Again'.

WON'T GET FOOLED AGAIN.

If there is a key song on 'Who's Next', it is this lengthy call to arms that became the traditional show closer at Who concerts from this point onwards. Based on a clattering synthesizer riff that locks the group into a tight, rhythmic performance, 'Won't Get Fooled Again' is classic mid-period Who at their very best, Pete's block chords firmly in place, John swooping up and down his bass, Roger singing his heart out and Keith an almighty presence, albeit slightly more disciplined than usual in view of the song's inflexible structure.

With lyrics that address the futility of revolution when the conqueror is likely to become as corrupt as the conquered, the song inspired many a clenched fist, especially when Roger came careering in at the end of the lengthy instrumental passage, declaiming the 'bosses' and inciting the kind of scenes that left the Bastille in ruins. His scream before the final verse is one of the most volatile vocal eruptions ever recorded.

Pete: "It's really a bit of a weird song. The first verse sounds like a revolution song and the second like somebody getting tired of it. It's an angry anti-establishment song. It's anti people who are negative. A song against the revolution because the revolution is only a revolution and a revolution is not going to change anything at all in the long run, and a lot of people are going to get hurt."

Edited down from its original eight minutes and thirty seconds, 'Fooled Again' as a single reached number 9 in the UK charts and 10 in the US.

QUADROPHENIA

ORIGINAL UK ISSUE: TRACK 2657 013, RELEASED NOVEMBER 1973; CD: POLYDOR 831 072-2.
US: MCA2 10004; CD: MCAD 2-6895; GOLD ULTRADISC: UDCD 2-550.

The Who were often accused of being obsessed with their own history, and while 'obsessed' is too strong a word, there is no doubt that their experiences as a band – and a band's experiences of life – offered Pete Townshend a rich seam of subject matter to chronicle in his songs. No better example of this can be found in The Who's catalogue than in 'Quadrophenia' which brought together several essential elements of Townshend's style: the song cycle, the synthesizers he'd pioneered on 'Who's Next', adolescent frustration, the search for spiritual contentment and, especially here, an effort to try and make sense of his own past, especially the Mod experience which he'd observed in 1964 and which was so closely wrapped up in The Who's story. In doing so he produced a minor masterpiece, probably the most underrated Who album of all, and one which continues to fascinate new converts 20 years after its initial release.

Unfortunately, while the timing for the release of 'Tommy' was well-nigh perfect, 'Quadrophenia' arrived at a time when lengthy rock works such as this were beginning to lose their charm. In 1973 rock fans seemed less inclined to sit through and assimilate so much material at one stretch as they were in 1969. By 1976, of course, three minute explosions – courtesy of the punk vanguard – would be all the rage and works like 'Quadrophenia' roundly vilified; not that The Who hadn't blazed a trail with three minute explosions of their own, of course, but that was conveniently forgotten by their critics.

There were also problems playing 'Quadrophenia' live. At their best The Who were a free-flowing, high energy machine, capable of improvising at will and flying off at remarkable tangents, usually on the spur of the moment at Pete's whim. The backing tapes of synthesizer music needed to present a substantial chunk of 'Quadrophenia' authentically on stage dictated a different approach, a more rigid style which allowed little room for The Who to play together in the manner in which they excelled. When the tapes didn't gel with The Who, or The Who didn't gel with the tapes, or – even worse – when the tapes came in at the wrong time and threw everyone off balance, 'Quadrophenia' came crashing down, reducing Pete to a spluttering rage. The other three, eager to please but concerned that Pete occasionally aimed too high, grew equally frustrated. So, too, did the fans. Eventually, rather like 'Tommy', 'Quadrophenia' was edited down, and only four songs: '5.15', 'Drowned', 'Punk And The Godfather' and 'Love Reign O'er Me' survived as live pieces, though special mention must be made of 'Bell Boy', Keith's vocal spotlight which remained a crowd favourite while he was alive.

'Quadrophenia' is the story of the journey of a Mod, name of Jimmy, whose restlessness, frustration and ultimate disillusionment drive him almost to suicide. It takes in many Mod concerns – clothes, style, Brighton trips, pills and even a Who concert – and ends on a note of triumph when Jimmy somehow manages to free himself from the shackles of the cult. Each member of The Who has his own musical theme in 'Quadrophenia', and each represents one facet of Jimmy's 'quadrophonic' personality, although this aspect of 'Quadrophenia' is never fully explored. Of course, none of The Who were Mods at all really. Roger and John were rockers at heart, Keith was into surf music and wanted to be a beach boy, and Pete was an art student with an inquisitive mind who latched on to Mods at the suggestion of early manager Pete Meaden as a way to further the band's career. But this didn't stop Pete from observing the Mods' way of life, their rituals and dances, and sympathising with their attitudes. 'Quadrophenia' was his debt to the cult of Mod and, in many ways, the album has become something of a lasting Mod icon, one of very few in the Mod heritage.

'Quadrophenia' was immaculately packaged in a handsome black and white gatefold sleeve, complete with extensive liner notes telling Jimmy's story and a 22-page book of evocative b&w photographs illustrating his odyssey. Released to coincide with The Who's first global tour for well over a year, it reached No 2 in both the UK and US album charts.

A 'Gold' remastered disc was issued in the US but has a disappointing overall sound, and Roger has often complained about the mix of the original 'Quadrophenia'. His vocals seem consistently low while John's bass, on the other hand, is mixed consistently high. Long term Who plans call for a thorough remixing.

I AM THE SEA

Opening with the sound of the ocean, faint echoes of the four principal 'Quadrophenia' themes are heard before John's bass comes dancing in and the guitar takes over. The sea and storm effects are captured perfectly and, on a good stereo system, sound wonderfully realistic, better than any special effects recording. There is a dramatic, startling link into...

THE REAL ME

... in which Roger, as Jimmy, ponders over his own identity, casting blame on those whom he feels have let him down.

Unadulterated rock, lifting and descending with asymmetric drum patterns and sharp guitar chords, plus the brass section that features heavily throughout 'Quadrophenia'. Towards the end the guitar, which is never obtrusive, cuts out completely to allow Moon and Entwistle to carry the rhythm as only they can.

QUADROPHENIA

An instrumental piece that introduces the various themes, much as the 'Overture' did for 'Tommy'. The arrangements are surprisingly sophisticated, and the pounding 'Love Reign O'er Me' is as powerful as anything on the record.

CUT MY HAIR

One of the less memorable songs on the album in which Jimmy sings of his home life and the hopelessness of always trying to stay ahead of fashion. It closes with a news item about Mods and Rockers fighting on Brighton seafront read in the BBC's most formal manner by announcer John Curle.

THE PUNK AND THE GODFATHER

Arguably the best track on the album, 'The Punk And The Godfather' sees Jimmy come face to face with The Who – with Pete as the Godfather – and question his allegiance. Opening with a magnificent double tracked guitar chord riff and with echoes of 'My Generation' and crowd noise, the uptempo passage fades away for one of the most evocative, autobiographical asides ("I've lived your future out, by pounding stages like a clown") Pete has ever written, and which he sings in complete contrast to Roger's angry attack.

I'M ONE

Opens as a gentle, folksy ballad with finger picked guitar before the band join to bring the song into its own; about Jimmy's determination to retain his own identity regardless of what the crowd may think. With less synthesizer – and consequently less overdubs – than most of the other tracks on 'Quadrophenia' – 'I'm One' has a distinct live feel to it.

THE DIRTY JOBS

In complete contrast to the previous song, there is almost no guitar on this fast, uptempo track but plenty of synthesizer supporting Roger as he sings about class conflict in the workplace from the point of view of the junior at the bottom of the heap.

HELPLESS DANCER
(Roger's Theme)

A dramatic but lean operatic-style aria featuring a double tracked Roger over staccato piano chords, acoustic guitar and little else. Underarranged, short, and decidedly experimental in tone, this is the least Who-like piece on the album which is intended to reflect Jimmy's increasing political awareness, but as has been pointed out elsewhere, Mods took no interest in politics whatsoever so its sensibility is quite out of character. Not that this sort of logical argument ever really bothered Pete when it came to creating a song cycle...

IS IT IN MY HEAD

Opening with a snatch of 'The Kids Are Alright', this was one of the earliest songs Pete wrote for 'Quadrophenia', a medium paced ballad which speeds up on the chorus but which hasn't as strong a melody as most tracks on the album.

I'VE HAD ENOUGH

Somewhat over-reaching itself, this song opens as a driving rocker, then jerks into a different passage before a final section in which Roger sings along country-style accompanied only by Pete on banjo. There are several songs on 'Quadrophenia' that, like this, attempt to scale epic heights, including 'The Punk And The Godfather', 'Bell Boy' and 'Doctor Jimmy', but this one doesn't quite measure up because the sections don't mesh together quite so well.

5.15

The best known song on 'Quadrophenia' and a minor hit single, '5.15' relates Jimmy's extra-sensual experiences on the train from London to Brighton sandwiched between two city gents. A memorable riff, emphasised by a horn section, it was probably too raw to be a serious chart contender, but listen out for Keith imitating the sound of train wheels decelerating, an effect he also played when The Who performed '5.15' live, which they often did.

SEA AND SAND

Another rather disjointed song with several different sections and tempo changes that all boil down to Jimmy's deciding to sleep on the beach. There's a confusing false ending and during the final fade-out Roger echoes some lines from 'I'm The Face', the Mod anthem recorded by The Who when they were known as The High Numbers.

DROWNED

A tough blues-based rocker which The Who loved to play on stage for its relative simplicity compared with other 'Quadrophenia' tracks. There's some great piano work from Chris Stainton but the overall feel of the song seems incompatible with the rest of the album.

Pete: "This song should actually stand alone... (when we were recording) it rained so hard that the walls were flowing with sheets of water. Chris Stainton played piano in a booth and when the take was finished he opened the door and about 500 gallons gushed out!"

BELL BOY
(Keith's Theme)

A rare Keith Moon vocal, shared at times with Roger, but unquestionably his best effort in The Who's catalogue – and the actual drumming is no slouch either. Somehow Keith manages to pitch things

exactly right here, blending his usual comic persona with a wistful, nostalgic glance back to the Mod experience and how it died after the glories of Brighton beach. Of course in his heart of hearts, Keith was nothing more than an old-fashioned showman who'd do anything to raise a cheer: 'Bell Boy' was among his finest cheers.

DOCTOR JIMMY (including IS IT ME?, John's Theme)

A steamroller of a song and certainly the *magnum opus* on the album, although its relative complexity – it was really two songs in one – meant that The Who never really mastered a lasting stage version.

John Atkins: "... a towering, massive song that threatens to bludgeon all in its path with its verse and stature. Cast in the huge, grandiose style that only The Who could pull off without sounding pretentious and unwieldy... thrilling chord changes, dramatic verses and a sweeping synthesizer score. The chorus is instantly catchy but has longevity of appeal and there's enough change and variety in the arrangement to justify the length (7.59) of the song. Like on 'Bell Boy', the confidence and vigour of The Who burns through this ambitious song and, significantly, they never attempted anything quite like it again."

Pete: "All the songs from 'Quadrophenia' are meant to fit together, or at least all reflect the personality of one person – as a result they are all structured similarly. But 'Dr Jimmy' is the archetype, more so in fact than 'Quadrophenia' itself."

THE ROCK

A lengthy instrumental passage in which the four main themes in Quadrophenia are reprised in a different arrangement from the earlier 'Quadrophenia' track.

LOVE REIGN O'ER ME
(Pete's Theme)

Four resounding notes, descending into the abyss that is both a stormy sea and Jimmy's confusion, herald the best known theme from 'Quadrophenia' and a

song The Who continued to perform right up until the end of their career. 'Love Reign O'er Me' reaches for greater heights than simply the climax to Jimmy's tale, and – with love as an allegory for Him – becomes a prayer to the heavens seeking absolution and contentment. Epic in scale, epic in performance and a shattering climax to a richly rewarding listening experience.

QUADROPHENIA SOUNDTRACK

ORIGINAL UK ISSUE: POLYDOR 2625 037, RELEASED SEPTEMBER 1979; CD: POLYDOR 519 999-2. US: POLYDOR PD2-6235; CD: POLYDOR 314 519 999-2.

The soundtrack to the film *Quadrophenia* includes a selection of tracks remixed from the original double LP, three new Who songs included in the film but not on the original LP, 'Zoot Suit' by The High Numbers, and a side of music by various artists used in the soundtrack.

ZOOT SUIT
(P. Meaden)

The B-side of 'I'm The Face' is actually the melody of a song by The Showmen called 'Country Fool' with new lyrics by Pete Meaden designed to appeal to The Who's Mod following. The High Numbers take the song at a cracking pace, Pete sounds like a jazz guitarist and Roger's vocals are answered by the band Merseybeat style. As in all four High Numbers tracks that have been commercially released, Keith's drums are mixed too low.

GET OUT AND STAY OUT

With the title line repeated endlessly, this track makes its point in the movie – Jimmy's parents are chucking him out of the family home – but on record it's more than a tad tedious. Obviously written to accompany film action.

FOUR FACES

With Pete on vocals backed by his own piano, this song finds Jimmy pondering his quadrophonic personality after being thrown out. Pleasant and tuneful but lightweight compared to the real 'Quadrophenia' material.

JOKER JAMES

An odd little song about James the practical joker whose odd sense of humour costs him girlfriend after girlfriend when he inflicts them to the joys of whoopee cushions and itching powder. If Pete wasn't credited with writing this, most Who watchers would swear it was an Entwistle song, at least by the lyrics.

ODDS AND SODS

ORIGINAL UK ISSUE: TRACK 2406 116, RELEASED OCTOBER 1974; UK CD: POLYDOR 517 946-2. US: MCA 2126; CD: MCAD-1659.

'Odds And Sods' was The Who's attempt at clearing the decks. Over the years they'd recorded many songs that were never released, though some of them – notably 'Naked Eye' and 'Pure And Easy' – had been played live and were well known to fans. With time on his hands, John Entwistle started rooting around the tape boxes at Track Records and came up with a quite remarkable collection of songs which The Who had deemed unworthy of release, either because they simply didn't fit into the mood of whatever it was The Who were working on at the time or, in the case of material recorded for 'Lifehouse'/'Who's Next', there was simply a surfeit of songs.

In the case of certain songs, perhaps The Who thought that they might one day record a better version, but whatever the motives, it says much for the band that songs of this standard (which many acts would have killed for) were simply shelved.

'Odds And Sods' reached No 10 in UK and No 15 in US.

POSTCARD
(Entwistle)

Opening with a stabbing brass rift and the well used lie, 'Having a wonderful time, wish you were here', this is John's tongue-in-cheek road song which details the sights and sounds of the countries visited by The Who on recent tours set to an up-tempo rock rhythm. Originally intended for an EP that never happened.

NOW I'M A FARMER

Recorded for the same EP as 'Postcard', this is Pete's wistful ode to the joys of an outdoor life digging in the fields. "This track is from the period when The Who went slightly mad," he wrote in the accompanying liner notes. "We put out several records called 'Dogs'..." Only Roger, at home on his farm on the Kent/Sussex border, was likely to have identified with the outdoor life, though Keith shows a natural bent towards horticulture matters during his spoken fade-out.

PUT THE MONEY DOWN

An upbeat 'Lifehouse' outtake with a slow synthesizer break, this track falls short of the standards reached by any of the 'Who's Next' songs, though the message – a diatribe about the lack of relationship between artist and audience – comes across clearly enough. This track remained uncompleted until 1974 when Roger finally finished the vocal so it could be included on 'Odds And Sods'.

LITTLE BILLY

'Little Billy' is a stern anti-cigarette song The Who recorded on behalf of the American Cancer Society, with fairly grisly lyrics – for once Pete might have been inspired by John – that really do suggest that smoking can kill. Considering that all four members of The Who were heavy smokers at this time, it was somewhat hypocritical but it's an entertaining narrative piece which the ACS declined to use on the grounds that it was too frightening.

TOO MUCH OF ANYTHING

Another 'Lifehouse' outtake, 'Too Much Of Anything' is a rather pedestrian rock ballad with Nicky Hopkins on piano which deals with greed and its consequences, but the song meanders along indifferently without the punch of other 'Lifehouse' tracks. The Who occasionally played it on stage in 1971 but soon dropped it.

GLOW GIRL

The seeds of 'Tommy' lie in this pleasingly melodic track, Pete's second aeroplane crash song, which closes with 'Tommy's opening lines, albeit referring to a girl... 'It's a girl Mrs Walker...'.

Pete: "I wrote it because we were taking off in a plane which I seriously thought was going to crash, and as I was going up I was writing this list. I thought that if I was a chick and I was in a plane that was diving for the ground and I had my boyfriend next to me and we were on our honeymoon or we were about to get married, I know what I'd think of. I'd think about him and I'd think about what I am

going to be missing. So I went through this list... of what was in the chick's purse – cigarettes, Tampax – a whole lyrical list and then holding his hand and what he felt and was gonna say to her.

"He is a romanticist... he is trying to have some romantic and soaring last thoughts. Eventually what happens is they crash and they are reincarnated that instant musically... they've been re-incarnated as this girl. 'It's a girl, Mrs Walker, it's a girl,' – that was supposed to be the end of the thing."

As it happened, it was merely the beginning of far greater things.

PURE AND EASY

A key song from the 'Lifehouse' project, 'Pure And Easy' is a beautiful Townshend ballad which ought to have appeared on 'Who's Next' but was left off, probably because The Who weren't 100% satisfied with the version they'd recorded during the 'Lifehouse'/'Who's Next' sessions and which appears here. It's Pete's re-write on the myth of the 'Lost Chord', a deeply-felt song about the ultimate musical note, the loss of which symbolises mankind's decaying relationship with the universe. It is a song of yearning, almost a tearful lament, albeit fashioned over Who style torrents. The guitar solo builds to a tremendous climax, rather like Jimmy Page's memorable solo in 'Stairway To Heaven'.

Pete thought very highly of 'Pure And Easy' when he wrote it, so much so that its chorus forms a coda to 'Song Is Over' on 'Who's Next', and he included it in demo form on his first solo album 'Who Came First'.

It is remarkable to think that at this stage in his evolution as a songwriter (1971), Pete Townshend was able to discard material as strong as this. The Who performed 'Pure And Easy' briefly during 1971.

FAITH IN SOMETHING BIGGER

An early, unsophisticated (even for 1968) attempt by Pete to express his growing devotion to Him. Charming vocal harmonies but unsubtle and, by The Who's own standards, rather naïve.

I'M THE FACE

'I'm The Face' was the first record released by The Who, or The High Numbers as they were then called. A Mod rallying cry with lyrics by their then manager Pete Meaden set to the melody of Slim Harpo's 'Got Love If You Want It', it failed to make the charts but the original single on the Fontana label has since become – along with 'Who Did It'*, the album that never was – the best known and most valuable collectors' item in the band's entire catalogue. Mint condition singles can set you back almost £200. Rumour has it that only 1,000 were pressed, and a good quantity of them were apparently bought up by John Entwistle's grandmother.

Thirty years on 'I'm The Face' rocks out with all the raw enthusiasm of a teenage band on the first rung of the pop ladder, and although Keith is subdued by later standards, John and Pete display embryonic Who tendencies behind Roger's giddy shout.

[* 'Who Did It' featured Side one from

'A Quick One' on one side and Side two from 'The Who Sell Out' on the other. Although it was never released, a few copies somehow got out in the early Eighties.]

NAKED EYE

A superb stage song, 'Naked Eye' was never captured properly in the studio and this version remained the only one extant until a better but still imperfect live recording turned up on 'Maximum R&B'. 'Naked Eye' was played at virtually every Who concert in the early Seventies, and took on enormous power as Pete and Roger shared verses that contained some of Pete's most powerful lyrical imagery ever. Between oblique references to drugs and guns is a deep sense of frustration and failure, of not knowing where next to run to, yet at the time realising that to stand still is suicidal, matters uppermost in Pete's mind as he sought to justify his continued role in The Who and The Who's continued existence. Meanwhile the band strains at the leash, while a strange nagging riff holds the song together. This riff made its first appearance at concerts during 1969 when the band were jamming at the climax to their shows and only later did Pete add lyrics to harness it into 'Naked Eye'.

Like 'Pure And Easy', 'Naked Eye' is an essential Who song, far more important than many found elsewhere in the catalogue. That it was condemned to this album seems like either resigned indifference or artistic suicide by its writer.

LONG LIVE ROCK

Featured in the film *That'll Be The Day*, in which Keith Moon made his acting début, and sung by Billy Fury, 'Long Live Rock' was originally written as part of an album about the history of The Who, a concept that Pete abandoned in favour of 'Quadrophenia'. Reminiscent of Fifties' style rock and roll with its jangly piano and almost-12-bar arrangements, Pete sings lead and makes several sideways references to headline-grabbing aspects of The Who's story. A fine rocker; whoever said that Keith couldn't keep proper time should listen hard to his one.

Original Soundtrack Recording

Featuring: Eric Clapton/Roger Daltrey/John Entwistle/Elton John/Ann-Margret
Keith Moon/Jack Nicholson/Oliver Reed/Pete Townshend/Tina Turner/The Who

T the Movie mmy

Polydor

A two-record set

TOMMY SOUNDTRACK LP

ORIGINAL UK ISSUE: POLYDOR 2657 014, RELEASED MARCH 1975; UK CD: POLYDOR 841 121-2.
US: POLYDOR PD2-9505; CD: POLYDOR 841 121-2.

Not strictly a Who album, though all four members of The Who are featured on the reworked versions of 'Tommy' songs as they appeared in the movie. There's an interesting selection of vocalists, including Oliver Reed (whose singing voice makes Keith sound like a choirboy), Jack Nicholson (who couldn't sing either), Tina Turner (whose 'Acid Queen' is terrific), Ann-Margret and Elton John, whose spin through 'Pinball Wizard' with his own stage band is the album's highlight and which became a hit single for him. By and large, the songs all feature an abundance of Pete's synthesizer work and elaborate choral arrangements by backing vocalists brought in to offset the musical shortcomings of tone deaf actors.

Several songs are radically reworked by the all-star band (which, ironically, includes Kenney Jones on drums on many of the tracks since Keith couldn't be relied upon), and there are a couple of completely new songs in 'Champagne' and 'Mother And Son'. John does most of the bass work and as well as playing all the synthesizers Pete also produced the record, a thankless chore – in retrospect – that drove him to the brink of another nervous breakdown.

This LP is really a kitsch novelty item of interest only to Who academics. Stick to The Who's version, or better still, seek out live versions of the 'Tommy' material by The Who *circa* 1969/70.

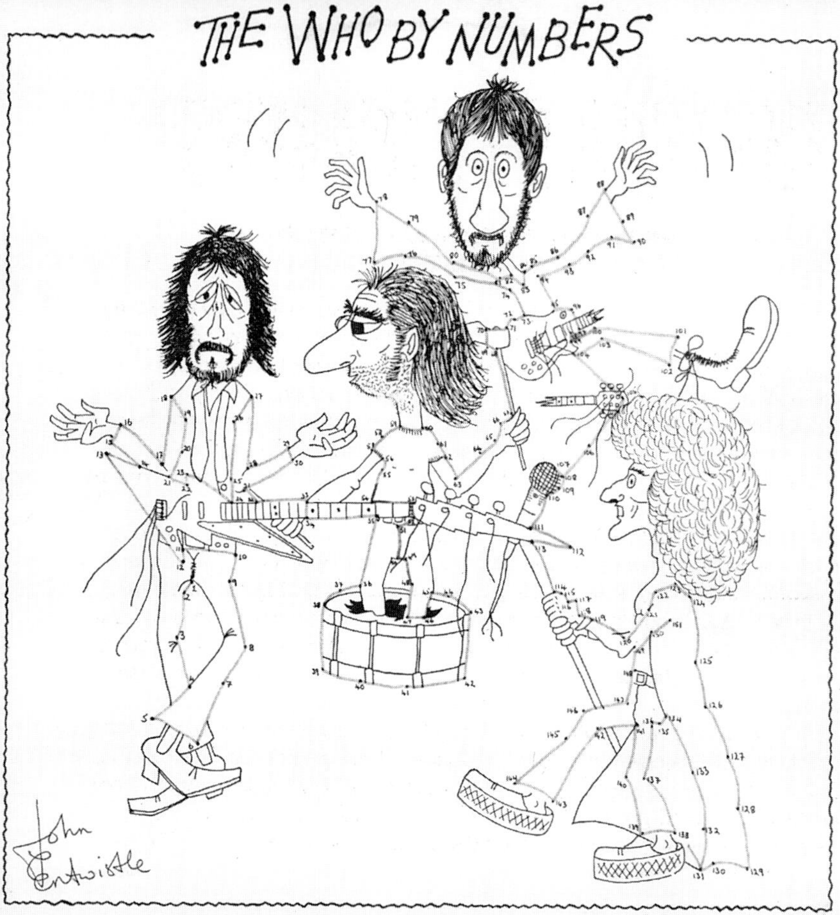
THE WHO BY NUMBERS
John Entwistle

THE WHO BY NUMBERS

ORIGINAL UK ISSUE: POLYDOR 2490 129, RELEASED OCTOBER 1975; CD: POLYDOR 831 522-2.
US: MCA 2161; CD: MCAD 37002.

By the time the group got around to recording 'The Who By Numbers', they were tired, insecure and feeling the pace, and although this record was never intended as a concept album, there is a running theme of discontent, disillusionment and, above all, the dilemma of growing old in the band that once sang about hoping to die first. It was almost as if Pete approached this stage in The Who's career as a penitent might approach the confession box; never one to shrink from the truth, on 'Who By Numbers' Pete lays bare his soul and the demons that lay within, and it didn't always make for fun listening.

Overall, 'The Who By Numbers' has a much lighter sound than any of its predecessors. Here Townshend abandons the synthesizers of 'Who's Next' and 'Quadrophenia' and eschews his trademark block chords for diligent lead guitar. Keith's drums rarely pound as they once did and Roger's voice, becoming deeper but more sonorous as it aged, no longer spits out Townshend's words with the ferocity of old. Only John retains his trademark bass-style, fast and fluid and, on 'Dreaming From The Waist', in a class of his own.

At this point in their career The Who on record and The Who live became two different entities. Only two of the new songs here – 'Squeeze Box' and 'Dreaming From The Waist' – were played with any regularity in a live set that gradually became a celebratory and vigorously performed parade of former glories, though 'Slip Kid' and 'However Much I Booze' were tried on stage and soon discarded. On its release The Who made

a triumphant return to the stage, touring the US with the same zest and expertise that they showed five years earlier, but deep inside Townshend knew that to survive as a creative vehicle, and therefore retain his interest, The Who had to change – or stagnate. The problem was the direction in which to change and the expectations of fans who liked their Who loud and brash, just as they always had been.

But there was still much to laud on 'Who By Numbers': 'Slip Kid', 'Dreaming From The Waist' and 'Imagine A Man' were all first rate songs; 'Success Story' was good enough to have succeeded 'My Wife' as a stage vehicle for John; ' Squeeze Box' was fun; and 'Blue, Red And Grey' was as charming a solo piece as Pete had ever recorded.

Clad in a self-deprecatory join-up-the-dots cartoon design by John, it reached number 7 in UK and 8 in the US.

SLIP KID

An eight-beat count-in leads into a shuffle rhythm that could be a drum machine, before Roger and Pete swap autobiographical lines about a rock'n'roll kid who's lost when he grows up. With Roger singing 'There's no easy way to be free', and Pete rejoining 'It's a hard hard world', the mood of the album is immediately apparent. Nicky Hopkins is featured on piano and there's a fine guitar solo.

HOWEVER MUCH I BOOZE

One of the distinctive aspects of 'The Who By Numbers' is that songs of personal anguish are couched in pleasant, almost cheerful melodies. Here, while Pete sings lyrics about his failures and vanities, reaching the conclusion that 'There's no way out', the band skip along lightly and Pete adds some authentic country style picking during his solo. The short, slow middle-eight is charmingly sung.

SQUEEZE BOX

An uncharacteristically jolly song with lascivious undertones, 'Squeeze Box' is a most un-Who-like tumble into uncomplicated rolling rhythms enlivened by Pete as multi-instrumentalist on accordion and banjo as well as guitar, though the ending, with the tremolo chord, is classic Who. 'Squeeze Box' became a minor hit single for The Who, reaching number 10 in the UK and 16 in the US.

Pete: "I went out and bought an accordion and learned to play it in about ten minutes, so it's a devastatingly simple song."

DREAMING FROM THE WAIST

Pete has said he hated playing this track, mainly because of the tricky opening chords high up on the fretboard, but with its tumbling rhythm, melodic, harmony-clad chorus and general sizzle, it ranks with many of The Who's best ever songs. It also offers John an opportunity to stretch out: his popping bass solo in the closing bars is a stunning display of virtuosity which he'd play live with the casual aplomb of the player whose fingers other bassists would kill for.

IMAGINE A MAN

With an introduction not unlike 'Behind Blue Eyes', 'Imagine A Man' is a dramatic ballad with a lovely, distinctive melody and profound lyrics about the tedium of day-to-day life, something that rock stars are not supposed to know much about. Townshend kept in touch with the street more than most, however, and his observations are keenly felt.

SUCCESS STORY
(Entwistle)

The malaise that affected Pete had its effect on John as well, for the message of this catchy autobiographical rocker seems to be that being a member of The Who used to be fun but no longer is. John's songs rarely slotted into whatever theme occupied Pete's mind when The Who were recording but this time he was spot on. "I may go far... if I smash my guitar," can only have been written about Townshend. John contributes a great hook line throughout.

THEY ARE ALL IN LOVE

The lightest – and prettiest – song on the album again speaks of disillusionment and cynicism, with a melodious Roger and gentle piano disguising bitter sentiments about the music industry.

Pete: "The song was about what the band has become. It was about money, about law courts, about lawyers and accountants. Those things had never mattered and then the band had a backlog of tax problems and unpaid royalties. We had to deal with it. I really felt like crawling off and dying."

BLUE RED AND GREY

In which Pete, accompanying himself on ukulele and unsupported by the rest of the band, declaims the millionaire lifestyle in favour of the virtues of a simple life. An uncomplicated melody, performed with the kind of tongue-in-cheek sincerity which Pete had previously demonstrated on his first solo album 'Who Came First'. The brass band adds to the sense of poignancy. Utterly charming.

HOW MANY FRIENDS

Surrounded by sycophants who never say what they really mean, Pete's misery knows no bounds but as Dave Marsh observed in his Who biography *Before I Get Old*, Townshend probably enjoyed the company of fewer sycophants and yes-men than most rock stars, and many of his oldest friends who stuck around were as outspoken as he was. Of course, the same could not be said for Keith who attracted legions of hangers-on that laughed like trained hyenas every time the hapless drummer opened his mouth.

Roger takes the vocals on a bitter, piano-based song.

IN A HAND OR A FACE.

With Roger sounding as bitter as ever in a final slab of self-pity, this song is pinned together by a repetitive three chord riff, but it's below par musically for the album's closer, rather anonymous and highlighted only by Pete's lively solo and a brief drum break. Because of the poor quality of production compared to the rest of the album, this song appears to have been slapped on the end almost as an afterthought.

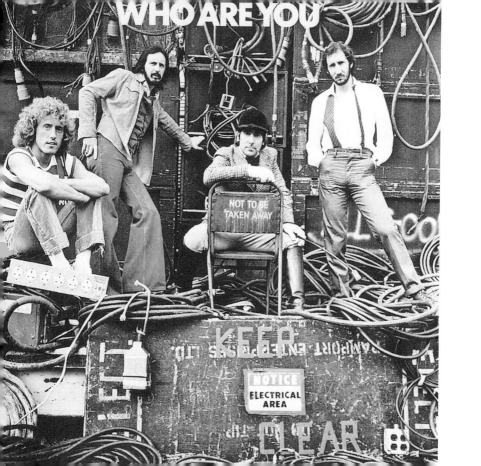

WHO ARE YOU

ORIGINAL UK ISSUE: POLYDOR 2490 147 WHOD 5004, RELEASED AUGUST 1978; UK CD: POLYDOR 831 557-2. US: MCA 3050; CD: MCAD 37003; 'GOLD' CD: MCA UD CD 561.

Inertia never suited The Who. They thrived on fast paced energy and produced their best work in a hurry. Three years between the release of 'Who By Numbers' and 'Who Are You' was the longest gap ever between Who releases and in the meantime much had occurred, none of it likely to benefit the group. They'd never been the closest of colleagues outside of the recording studio and the stage, but during these three years they'd grown apart in so many ways that they no longer resembled anything remotely like the gang they'd once been. Pete's spiritual and intellectual quests were ongoing but frustrating and his musings were quite alien to Roger, the practical landowner who just wanted to get on with his job and not philosophise about it; John was simply a very skilled professional musician who wanted and needed to work regularly; Keith, his marriage now over, was sick with alcoholism, lonely and desperate for something besides the disintegrating Who to fill an empty life.

Pete knew that the only way the group could survive was to steer them in new directions. The other three resisted the insecurity of change. Given half the chance Pete would have broken up the group before 'Who Are You' was recorded, but he felt a loyalty to his three colleagues, especially Keith, and soldiered on regardless. The result is a transitional album based largely around synthesizer patterns that could have pointed the way to the future were it not for Keith dying within a month of its release. In a stylistic shift that would become more apparent later, the arrangements of the songs – and the songs themselves – are more complex than ever before, and they tend to meander where once they had taken the direct route. As would also become the pattern in future, John's songs take greater prominence, and Roger sings an Entwistle song.

Moon's accidental but tragically predictable death, completely overshadowed the release of 'Who Are You'. Ironically, he is photographed on the cover sitting on a chair with the words 'Not To be Taken Away' on its back; the other irony is that on one song, 'Music Must Change', Keith didn't play drums because he couldn't handle its unusual tempo. "But I'm the best Keith Moon style drummer in the world," he is reported to have told Pete when he couldn't play it, but either way Moon wasn't firing on all cylinders throughout the recording and it shows, but perhaps this is what Pete might have wanted. Moon, more than any of his three colleagues, represented the thundering recklessness of the old style – and younger – Who. But although his death freed them from the grip of the past, the future, as the final two albums demonstrated, turned out to be a barren land all the same, creatively at least.

'Who Are You' reached number 6 in UK and 2 in US. The US 'Gold' CD contains an alternative version of 'Guitar And Pen' as a bonus track.

NEW SONG

With synthesizers as the dominant instrument throughout the album, it's appropriate that they should open the first song, an upbeat, unconventional sounding rocker that bemoans the repetitive nature of rock as a whole and The Who in particular. "We sing the same old song," sings Roger but with less cynicism than on the previous album. That the song tends to drag can be put down to Keith's lack of energy, a sad state of affairs that was never truly remedied.

HAD ENOUGH
(Entwistle)

The first of two John Entwistle songs that he wrote for a science fiction fantasy that was originally intended to become a solo album. Here it is sung by Roger and dominated by synthesizer, from the intro to the maudlin sweeping strings in the solo that sound rather like the soundtrack to an epic western. There's also a brass interlude from John, and Roger's vocals on the chorus are eminently listenable.

905
(Entwistle)

The second sci-fi fantasy song, carried forth by a bip-bopping synthesizer features John singing the autobiography of a robot, but it's lost in the drabness of the tune.

SISTER DISCO

Synthesizers again dominate this fairly well known upbeat rocker sung by Roger which has little to do with disco music but more to do with fans, a subject Pete is drawn to again and again. As ever Pete comes in to sing a slower middle-eight, and he contributes some nice picking in the solo and chord work at the end. 'Sister Disco' became a popular stage number for the new look Who that emerged after Keith Moon's death.

MUSIC MUST CHANGE

Keith was unable to play the tricky time signature on this track which isn't surprising as it's no foot-tapper. It meanders through verses at a shuffle, then breaks out into experimental jazz tempos of uncharacteristic complexity for The Who. Once again, Pete comes in to sing a softer refrain at odds with the verses. The message here is heartfelt: Pete wanted music to change which is what the punk rockers were saying as well, but any punk listening to this elaborate piece of art rock would have thrown up within seconds.

TRICK OF THE LIGHT
(Entwistle)

John's multi-stringed bass dominates an uptempo song about a night with a prostitute to the extent that everyone and everything else in the studio is pretty superfluous. Murky stuff.

GUITAR AND PEN

Another experimental song with Roger's vocals on the operatic side and the unison chorus sounding vaguely like the chorus line from a Gilbert & Sullivan comic opera. Midway through the song descends into a free-form solo and it's clear that this is the kind of material Pete enjoyed writing at the time, whether The Who liked it or not. I doubt whether Keith did. The 'Gold' CD offers an alternative version, even more mannered than this cut.

(There's another, better example of this writing style on 'Rough Mix', the album that Pete recorded with Ronnie Lane in 1976/77, called 'Street In The City'. Indeed, 'Rough Mix' contains at least two Townshend songs, 'My Baby Gives It Away' and 'Keep Me Turning', which are better than almost all the material that Pete recorded with The Who from this point onwards. The sooner 'Rough Mix' is available on CD the better.)

LOVE IS COMING DOWN

A slow ballad with a rather slushy MOR string arrangement swells up on the choruses but goes nowhere in particular.

WHO ARE YOU.

One day in March 1977 Pete spent more hours that he cared to remember in a meeting to sort out The Who's tangled financial affairs and came away at the end with a cheque for seven figures. Most people would have been delighted at this outcome, but Pete was disgusted with himself. He was a musician, not a businessman. So he got drunk as hell at The Speakeasy, the London rockbiz club, where he encountered two Sex Pistols who pronounced themselves Who fans. This only aggrieved Pete more, so he tore up the cheque. When he left the club he was pie-eyed, and he slumped into a doorway, where he spent the night. At dawn he was awoken by a policeman who recognised him, and sent him on his way. This story forms the lyrical basis for 'Who Are You'.

The musical basis is the lengthy prologue, mid-section, and close, in which the title is repeated in a looping synthesizer-propelled chant similar to that used by middle eastern Sufi dancers as they near a trancelike state. Although it ebbs and flows, and at one point Pete plays an acoustic refrain, it embodies all the energy of past Who classics and at over six minutes is far and away the most arresting track on the album. Even Keith manages to keep up the tempo on this one.

In concert Roger frequently ad-libbed 'Who the fuck are you' and, during the lengthy mid-section, demonstrated his physical fitness by running on the spot for what seemed like ages. Although its message is unclear, 'Who Are You' is unquestionably the last great Who song the group recorded.

THE KIDS ARE ALRIGHT

ORIGINAL UK ISSUE: POLYDOR 2675 179, RELEASED JUNE 1979; UK CD: POLYDOR 517 947-2. US: MCA2 11005; CD: MCAD 6899.

The double LP of the 'soundtrack' of *The Kids Are Alright* film contains material that doesn't actually appear on the film, while the soundtrack itself contains material that doesn't appear on this album. Certain tracks on the LP were identical to the original releases, and in the movie The Who lip-synced to these songs. The album was produced by John Entwistle and taken from various film clips, regular releases and special performances staged for the film. It offered fans a number of alternative versions of previously released material, mainly live cuts, many of which, especially 'Sparks', 'See Me Feel Me', 'Baba O'Riley' and 'Won't Get Fooled Again', were exceptionally well performed.

The track listing is as follows: Side One: My Generation, from *The Smothers Brothers* TV show; I Can't Explain, from the *Shindig* TV show; Happy Jack, recorded live at Leeds University, not in the film; I Can See For Miles, from *The Smothers Brothers* TV show, not in the film; Magic Bus, regular studio version; Long Live Rock, regular studio version; Side Two: Anyway, Anyhow, Anywhere, from *Ready Steady Go!;* Young Man Blues (Allison), from the London Coliseum, 1969; My Wife (Entwistle), live from Kilburn State Theatre, London, December 15, 1977, not in the film; Baba O'Riley, live from Shepperton Studios, May 25, 1978; Side Three: A Quick One, live from Rolling Stones *Rock'n'Roll Circus* filming, Wembley, December 11, 1968; Tommy Can You Hear me, regular studio version; Sparks, live from Woodstock;

Pinball Wizard, live from Woodstock; See Me Feel Me, live from Woodstock; Join Together/Road Runner/My Generation Blues, live from Pontiac Silverdome, Michigan, December 6, 1975; Won't Get Fooled Again, live from Shepperton Studios, May 25, 1978.

'Kids' reached number 26 in the UK, number 8 in US.

FACE DANCES

ORIGINAL UK ISSUE: POLYDOR 2302 106 WHOD 5037, RELEASED MARCH 1981; CD: POLYDOR 517 948-2;
US: WARNER BROS WB HS3516; CD: WB: 3516-2; REISSUED ON MCA: MCAD 25-25987.

After Keith's death The Who became a different band and the two albums they made with Kenney Jones on drums sound like it. The greatest difference is what appears to be a lack of direction, even a lack of conviction, but the blame for this cannot be laid at Jones' feet. Pete was no longer saving his best material for The Who – his solo albums took preference – and the songs he gave Roger to sing with the band seemed too wordy, too autobiographical and altogether unsuited to his style of singing. Additionally, Pete's melodies were complex and often convoluted, as if he were trying too hard to impress, and they often relied too heavily on synthesizers rather than guitar. The Who sounded heavy only on John Entwistle's songs, but it was a leaden, lumpy kind of heavy-metal heaviness, lacking interesting melodies and quite unlike the springy, alert sound of the best hard rock songs that Pete – and occasionally John – were writing at the beginning of the decade. On Pete's songs the music was light and the words often seem out of sync, while John's contributions sounded like another band altogether and just confused matters even more.

  Although Keith's drumming had deteriorated on the final two Who albums he played on, his peculiar up-front style was an integral part of their sound which helped the melody along on many of their best songs. Jones was a steady, on the beat drummer, eminently professional by anyone's standards, but these abilities were not in line with The Who's glorious past and never would be. Now The Who were just another rock band, indeed a very good one live, but no longer did they stand out from the pack, at least not on record.

John sums up the situation better than anyone: "The last two Who albums are a kind of blank. By the time we were recording them, personalities were clashing. There were different ideas of music policy. General backbiting. People not agreeing with each other. Roger and Pete always had differing opinions about everything, but myself and Keith would make our minds up and, usually, things went in the way that myself and Keith wanted, so we never got into four-piece arguments usually. After Keith died, those were the hardest times..."

'Face Dances', produced by Bill Szymczyk, was released at a time when the new look Who launched themselves in a barrage of publicity which probably explains why it leapt to number 2 in UK album charts and number 4 in the US. The new Who toured excessively in the two years following Jones' arrival, but the show they presented relied almost entirely on past glories. When they played material from 'Face Dances', many fans took the opportunity to go for a drink. Aside from Jones, there were other changes in the traditional Who *modus operandi*: John 'Rabbit' Bundrick played keyboards on stage and played them well, and on some of the newer numbers Roger played guitar on stage for the first time since the days of The Detours in 1962.

Pete's song 'Face Dances', incidentally, was never released by The Who. Pete recorded it for his 'All the Best Cowboys Have Chinese Eyes' album. A shame – it's better than almost everything on this album.

YOU BETTER YOU BET

The best known song on the album, the one that was deservedly chosen for a single, opens with a popping synthesizer line and features several Who trademarks: changes in tempo, rumbling bass runs and some powerful upfront singing from Roger who is clearly responding well to the challenge of a Moonless band. Indeed, Roger's accent sounds more like that of the traditional Londoner he is than ever before.

The best track on 'Face Dances' by a country mile, it reached number nine in the UK singles charts.

DON'T LET GO THE COAT

Opening with a riff that sounds for all the world like an American AOR band, 'Don't Let Go' switches between a gentle rolling rhythm and a tempo that for The Who could almost be described as funky. Neither sounds like The Who of old and Roger struggles with a lyric inspired by Meher Baba's instructions to his followers not to abandon his 'robe', an allegory for his teachings. But the singer seems to be apologising for his inadequacy, his unworthiness, which doesn't suit Roger's *braggadocio* style.

CACHE CACHE

Similar in tempo to 'You Better You Bet' but lacking the energy and veering off at slower tangents, this is a rather dull song with curious lyrics inspired by a nocturnal visit to Vienna Zoo which saw Pete join the bears in their cage. Lifted by a great guitar solo, but still lacklustre and, even with a lyric sheet, difficult to comprehend.

THE QUIET ONE
(Entwistle)
Still waters run deep according to this autobiographical slab of heavy metal sung in a raucous but rather tuneless tone by John after smoking several packs of fags. This rocks along with the balls of 'My Wife' but without the interesting changes or power chords. John often sang this on stage following the album's release.

DID YOU STEAL MY MONEY

An untypical jerky time signature dominates an undistinguished tune in which the title is repeated too many times for comfort. Forgettable.

HOW CAN YOU DO IT ALONE?

Pete Townshend might have written rock operas but he was never known for writing story songs, at least not until this stage in his career as a writer, but 'How Can You Do It Alone' certainly contains the most interesting lyrics on 'Face Dances', set to a slap-bang tempo. It's about life's down-and-outs, as encountered by Pete, but the complexities of the verses are again incompatible with Roger's vocal style and the message of the song – show sympathy for losers – gets lost in the elaborate arrangement. The peculiar martial rhythms in the middle don't help either.

DAILY RECORDS

Again, this autobiographical song about ageing and trying to keep up with musical fashion just doesn't suit Roger's voice and, apart from the great jangly guitar solo, lacks conviction as a result.

YOU
(Entwistle)

Roger sings John's second HM-style contribution, a song about a reluctant Romeo anxious to avoid further entanglements in case the consequences prove as expensive as previous affairs. Fast and furious, like 'The Quiet One', and enlivened in part by John's riffing on what sounds like an eight-string bass guitar.

ANOTHER TRICKY DAY

'Another Tricky Day' closes the album on a lyrically pessimistic note, although the song itself is more interesting than most on 'Face Dances' and was played live on the tours that followed.

IT'S HARD

ORIGINAL UK ISSUE: POLYDOR WHOD 5066, RELEASED SEPTEMBER 1982; CD: POLYDOR 800 106-2.
US: WARNER BROS WB 23731; CD: WARNER BROS WB 23731-2.

It's difficult to get away from the notion that The Who's final album was recorded purely because they owed it to their American record company who'd paid them a substantial advance which might have had to be returned if no album was forthcoming.

'It's Hard' suffers from all the same problems as 'Face Dances', only more so: there's no unity between lyrics and melody, the music is irritatingly bitty and light, the songs are ineffective, Roger isn't suited to sing them and John Entwistle's tracks again sound like the work of a different act altogether.

Pete was no longer interested. His own solo albums were superior affairs and it's really no surprise that the best track on 'It's Hard', 'Eminence Front', is actually more of a Townshend solo effort than a band recording. The rest are a grab-bag of second-raters, often bland and confusing or both, always lacking power and nothing less than a pale shadow of the songs he wrote a decade before.

Released to coincide with what was billed as The Who's farewell tour of America, which included two nights at Shea Stadium in New York, it reached number 11 in UK and 8 in US.

ATHENA

A promising rumble that echoes the old Who opens the album in encouraging fashion, especially as Roger and Pete exchange vocals and Pete slows down the tempo to sing a middle-eight. A stabbing brass section dodges in and out of the chorus and Kenney Jones lets rip with a few drum rolls, but 'Athena', whoever she might be, remains out of reach.

IT'S YOUR TURN
(Entwistle)

In what was now becoming a habit, Roger sings an Entwistle song, and in a curious way John's songs seem more appropriate to his style than many of those that Pete was sending his way. Here there's a dense backing track but the song strides along at a solid rock tempo, featuring Andy Fairweather Low on rhythm guitar, which suggests Pete wasn't around when it was recorded. The song is about ageing, and passing on the baton to the next generation of rock and rollers.

COOKS COUNTY

With an odd time signature, convoluted backing and difficult to decipher lyrics that seem to be about human suffering, this song never settles down and is quite forgettable. Particularly unsuitable for Roger.

IT'S HARD

Even Roger, eternally The Who's upfront flag waver and source of energy, seems to have lost his enthusiasm here. The vocals drag and, despite an upbeat chorus, so does the song. As the title implies, this is a song about life being tough, and it must have been in the studio when they recorded this cliché ridden effort. It was played on stage with Roger on guitar.

DANGEROUS
(Entwistle)

Synthesizers and John's twangy bass dominate another dense and rather lumpy anonymous rocker which was also performed on stage.

EMINENCE FRONT

The best song on the album and the least Who-like of them all, 'Eminence Front' has a tense, springy tempo underlined by synthesizer patterns and a nagging little riff that carries the slight but catchy melody. Some nice, loose guitar lines thread their way in and out but with no block chords, no Roger (he played guitar when Pete sang this one on stage), and no outstanding bass line, it's as if this was an entirely different band from the one that played the last track. This, of course, is probably what Pete wanted for his song about putting on a façade to hide behind.

I'VE KNOWN NO WAR

Synthesizer dominates Pete's musings on the end of World War II and his birth exactly twelve days after the Germans surrendered. Roger again seems unsuited to sing this but the monotonous pace doesn't help. Melodically uninteresting, the song just doesn't go anywhere at all.

ONE LIFE'S ENOUGH

A very short experimental piece with Roger singing light-opera style over piano and synthesizer. Mannered and taken at a strict tempo, Roger must have wondered whether Pete was off his rocker when he offered material like this to The Who.

ONE AT A TIME
(Entwistle)

For only the second time in The Who's career, John gets three songs on an album, but all three come at the same tempo. This one opens with a slightly off key brass band, includes more synthesizers and features John on vocals singing about the woman troubles which seem to have plagued him ever since his bank balance went into the black.

WHY DID I FALL FOR THAT

There's a typical Who chord change midway through the solo in this otherwise anonymous piece, but where's the guitar? Bah! Quality control was clearly out to lunch as Pete dredged up songs as uninspired as this...

A MAN IS A MAN

... and this. Roger and Pete swap vocal lines on another slight, forgettable ballad which drags along until alternate lines speed up during the chorus. Eminently forgettable.

CRY IF YOU WANT

The final studio song The Who would record as a group for almost ten years is an unmelodious piece about past indiscretions with a difficult tempo that features military drum patters to build up the drama. Just as forgettable as so many other songs on this weak, insipid album.

WHO'S LAST

16
TRACK
LIVE DOUBLE

INCLUDING:
"MY GENERATION"
"CAN'T EXPLAIN"
"SUBSTITUTE"
AND MORE

WHO 1

LATER LIVE ALBUMS

WHO'S LAST
ORIGINAL UK ISSUE: MCA WHO 1, RELEASED DECEMBER 1984; CD: MCAD WHO1. US: MCA2 8018; CD: MCAD2-8018.

It's a crying shame The Who waited until 1984 to release a full-blown double LP designed to represent an entire concert. By this time they'd given up touring completely and this came out almost as an afterthought, although at one time there were plans, regrettably abandoned, to include retrospective material from the early Seventies.

This is a reasonably accurate reflection of the way the band sounded on their 1982 US tour, and by any standards apart from their own, they didn't sound bad at all. They'd become what Roger and John always wanted: a streamlined, professional, major league rock attraction, capable of selling out vast arenas to fans who wanted to hear a diet of classic songs from The Who's splendid back catalogue. Roger and John (and Kenney Jones) were happy to oblige; Pete wasn't but he went along anyway, knowing that creatively The Who was a dead duck.

Most of the crowds who came to see The Who in 1982 hadn't seen them before and knew nothing of the glorious spark that illuminated them in days gone by. The fans sang along to 'See Me Feel Me', punched the air to 'Won't Get Fooled Again' and played air guitars to 'My Generation', and they went home happy, well satisfied with what The Who had given them. The Who got well paid (at last!), so why should anyone complain?

Well, for starters it's a shoddy state of affairs when four sides of live material recorded when The Who was coasting should find its way on to the market legitimately, while at the same time there was very little live material available – 'Leeds' excepted – from the era when they genuinely were the greatest live rock act of their time. Secondly, this album was heard by younger critics of the band – not to mention younger potential fans with perceptive ears – who inevitably turned around and quite rightly asked what all the fuss was about. Thirdly, most of these tracks were taken from the show in Toronto that was released on video the previous year (see 'The Who Rocks America' below), so serious fans already had these live recordings on that soundtrack anyway. Older fans of the band with good memories just shook their heads in resignation. Even the packaging – a dodgy Union Jack cover in the UK and dull black and gold effort in the US – was rank. What had happened to quality control? Why would The Who willingly allow their reputation to be trashed in this way?

Didn't they care any more? Who knows?

Keith must have rolled over in his grave when he heard it.

JOIN TOGETHER

ORIGINAL UK ISSUE: VIRGIN VDT 102, RELEASED MARCH 1990, CD: CDVDT 102; US: MCA3-19501.

In the US 'Join Together' was a boxed double album package of the 1989 reunion tour, designed as a memento from that project and little else. It features Pete, Roger and John augmented by many other musicians – *two* drummers (which must have satisfied Keith), keyboards, an extra guitarist, brass section and choir – recorded live in America. It's been called the Las Vegas Who by their more cynical critics, and once again older fans cringed at what they heard. It didn't sell and hit the remainder bins within months of release.

But at least this time there was no attempt at trying to sound like what they had once been. Everybody accepted that this was an exercise in nostalgia and the prevailing mood on tour was mercifully free of angst as a result. In a heart-warming speech at Wembley Arena Pete admitted that the band on stage was no longer The Who and that they'd done this tour principally for the money, and it's difficult to argue with the fact that, deep down, The Who had served rock well over the years and deserved finally to reap the kind of rewards that many lesser bands had earned years ago.

For the record, the first half of the double album features a good selection of 'Tommy' songs, followed by Who hits in the second and, for the first time on record, a Pete solo song – 'Rough Boys' – essayed by the band. There's also a live rendition of 'I Can See For Miles' which the four man Who were never able to perform live because it required two guitars. Another first is Pete playing acoustic guitar on stage and some of his rhythmic chord work, especially on the early 'Tommy' tunes, is first rate, evidence indeed that while his songwriting talents might have waned over the years, his ability as a guitarist had, if anything, improved.

COMPILATIONS

Despite Keith Moon's remark that The Who would never be compiled into collections of previously issued material, few back catalogues have been pillaged as rapaciously as theirs. By 1993 it was possible to have bought in the UK alone six hits albums – two of them doubles – which offered very similar track listings. Add to this imports of slightly different hits albums put out by MCA in the US, not to mention Who compilations from elsewhere in the world, and the figure runs well into the teens. Many of them are badly mastered and one, a Spanish hits LP, even has a stage shot of Track stablemates Golden Earring on the cover. So much for quality control! On top of that Track Records repackaged numerous Who albums in their budget 'Backtrack' series during the Seventies.

Dealt with below are all UK and US compilation albums, with full track listings.

Details of individual songs which do not appear on any of the albums listed above, including many of The Who's greatest recordings, can be found under the compilation 'Meaty Beaty Big And Bouncy', which remains the best Who hits set ever, and on the individual 'rarities' albums.

The first ever Who compilation album was 'Magic Bus – The Who On Tour' [Decca 5064 (mono), Decca 75064 (stereo); US CD: MCAD 31333] released by MCA in the US in September 1968 to capitalise on interest in The Who generated by their extensive touring that year. The Who were quick to realise that their best chance of success was as a live band but with this release MCA unwittingly did their best to scupper their chances. For starters, it gave a totally false impression that it was a live album; even worse, several tracks were badly mastered, and the entire concept – sleeve design and packaging – was just plain awful, outdated and naïve. It could have seriously affected The Who's US reputation were it not so blatantly obvious to anyone who knew anything about The Who that they had absolutely nothing whatsoever to do with it. The Who were justifiably furious; these days George Michael's trying to get out of his Sony contract for a much lesser offence. (Full 'Magic Bus' track listing: Disguises, Run Run Run, Dr Jekyll And Mr Hyde, Can't Reach You, Our Love Was, Call Me Lightning, Magic Bus, Someone's Coming, Doctor! Doctor!, Bucket T, Pictures Of Lily.)

The first UK compilation album, 'Direct Hits' [Track 612 006 (mono); 613 006 (stereo); no CD] came out in November of 1968 and gathered together a rather motley collection of early singles, 'B' sides and album tracks. It was by no means comprehensive as far as the singles were concerned, lacking any Shel Talmy productions which makes it inadequate as a retrospective of The Who's career to date. (Full 'Direct Hits' track listing: Bucket T, I'm A Boy, Pictures Of Lily, Doctor! Doctor!, I Can See For Miles, Substitute, Happy Jack, The Last Time, In The City, Call Me Lightning, Mary Anne With The Shaky Hand [acoustic version], Dogs.)

At the third attempt, they got it right...

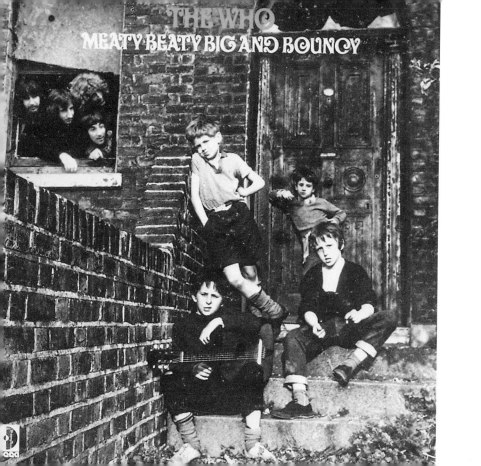

MEATY BEATY BIG AND BOUNCY

ORIGINAL ISSUE TRACK 1406 006; RELEASED OCTOBER 1971; NO CD. US: DECCA DL 79184, US CD: MCAD 37001.

'Meaty Beaty Big And Bouncy' was released simultaneously in the UK and US and did contain the Talmy sides (much to Kit Lambert's chagrin) and, with an attractive gatefold sleeve, remained the best Who retrospective on the market for a decade and a half. The running order was again chronologically awry but it went a long way towards introducing new American fans to The Who's early UK triumphs. In an article that Pete wrote for *Rolling Stone*, he described 'Meaty Beaty' as the best ever Who album, and he was probably right.

Full track listing: I Can't Explain, The Kids Are Alright, Happy Jack, I Can See For Miles, Pictures Of Lily, My Generation, The Seeker, Anyway Anyhow Anywhere, Pinball Wizard, A Legal Matter, Boris The Spider, Magic Bus, Substitute, I'm A Boy.

Tracks not dealt with above are as follows:

I CAN'T EXPLAIN

The Who's first single featured Jimmy Page on second guitar and The Ivy League on backing vocals and is an unashamed attempt at copying the riff style of The Kinks who were also produced by Shel Talmy. This similarity to The Kinks aside, 'Explain' was still an explosive début, a song about the frustration of being unable to express yourself, not just to the girl of your dreams but, in a broader sense, to the world as a whole. Roger spits out the words in sheer frustration while the band pound away, all of them aware that much depends on this song. Special mention is due to Keith, who announced his presence on the British pop scene with the kind of machine-gun drumming that was light years ahead of any of his peers.

In his Who biography *Before I Get Old*, Dave Marsh writes: "'I Can't Explain' is a slight song with a lyric on the edge of moony adolescent cliché, but as a recorded performance, it remains one of the outstanding documents of rock and roll. The sound is sharper, percussive, electric as a live wire. Voices ricochet off rim-shots, bass lines throb beneath guitar static. Roles are reversed: Moon's drums take short, shotgun solos, functioning similarly to conventional lead guitar. Townshend's guitar punches out its notes as if he's playing drum fills. Daltrey slurs the vocals in striking contrast to both the taut accents of the instruments and the precise punctuation of the chorus... (he) transforms the character of the moonstruck kid to a glaring, hostile Mod whose inarticulate state is a sound of rage and frustration."

Roger: "The Kinks were certainly a huge influence on Pete and he wrote 'I Can't Explain', not as a direct copy, but certainly it's very derivative of Kinks' music. I felt a bit uncomfortable when I had to sing it."

Perhaps the best testament to 'Explain' is that throughout their career, The Who almost always opened their live shows

with this song, occasionally alternating it with 'Substitute'. Is there any other band in the entire history of rock whose first single was so good, so timeless, that they could continue to use it as their opening number on stage for 25 years?

HAPPY JACK

When Cliff Townshend, Pete's dad, played saxophone in the RAF dance band The Squadronaires, the Isle of Man was a regular gig and Pete was dragged along, hence the Isle of Man reference in this great mid-Sixties Who single.

The star of the show here is Keith, whose remarkable drum patterns carry not only the beat, but, in a startlingly original fashion, the melody as well. All The Who's 1960s trademarks are present and correct: high harmonies, quirky subject matter, fat bass and drums that suspend belief.

At the end of the song Pete can be heard yelling 'I saw yer' to Keith who was trying to edge in on the vocals, now forbidden territory in view of his inability to sing on key.

PICTURES OF LILY

Never one to be coy in his choice of subject material, here's Pete's early observations on masturbation, written from the point of view of the young lad whose Dad sympathises with his jangling hormones and offers relief in the form of soft-core pictures. 'Lily' was quite daring for its time, and even today might likely generate a ban from sensitive radio stations and a headline in the tabloid press on a quiet news day, page three notwithstanding. Between the verses John steps forth on the French horn, which he played in a Boys' Brigade band in his early teens.

John: "It's all about wanking... Townshend going through his sexual traumas – something that he did quite often. I suppose you could say this record represents our smutty period, or to be more refined, our blue period."

'Lily' reached number 4 in the charts in 1967 and was the first single by The Who to be released on Track Records, the label formed by their co-managers Kit Lambert and Chris Stamp.

THE SEEKER

The Who were never a heavy metal band, but this track – with its 'heavy' repeated riff and rather lumbering rhythm track – comes close. But its introspective, yearning and evidently heart-felt lyrics are anything but heavy metal, and describe Pete's 'desperate' search for a meaning to his life, whether it be through his peers (references to Dylan, The Beatles) or drugs (Timothy Leary). The song was inspired by Pete's American friend Tom Wright, with whom he shared a flat in the early Sixties and whose record collection he inherited when Wright was busted for dope and deported. Wright went on to work for The Who and to manage rock venues in the US.

Either way, it was a poor choice for a single immediately after 'Tommy' and reached only number 19 in the UK and 44 in the US.

ANYWAY ANYHOW ANYWHERE
(Daltrey/Townshend)

The Who's second single slipped

between two tall stools, 'Explain' and 'Generation', but again allowed Roger the opportunity to spit out boastful lyrics about invincibility which, for the first and almost the last time on a Who song, he helped to write himself. What is most notable about 'Anyway' is the feedback noise guitar solo – in this instance coupled with Nicky Hopkins' rolling piano – which would be repeated to greater effect on 'Generation'. Here Pete was trying to bring The Who's stage act to the studio, trying to record The Who as they sounded live.

Pete: "I wrote the first verse and Roger helped with the rest. I was inspired by listening to Charlie Parker, feeling that this was really a free spirit, and whatever he'd done with drugs and booze and everything else, that his playing released him and freed his spirit, and I wanted us to be like that, and I wanted to write a song about that, a spiritual song."

'Anyway' made No 10 in the UK and, more importantly, was chosen as the theme tune for *Ready Steady Go!*, the groundbreaking weekly rock TV show on which The Who would be featured many times.

MAGIC BUS

This is the unedited and slightly different studio version of The Who's Bo Diddley influenced single; see 'Live At Leeds'. An edited version was released as a single in 1968.

SUBSTITUTE

Many fans' choice as the best Who single of all time, 'Substitute' is a timeless comment on image tampering, set to one of Pete's trickiest little riffs, all driven along by an omnipotent ringing open D string and – for the first time – that big fat *acoustic* sound he first heard on 'Three Steps To Heaven' by Eddie Cochran. Now a bona fide pop classic, 'Substitute' endured throughout The Who's live career, and was played at virtually every concert they ever performed.

Pete has stated that he felt The Who was a substitute for The Rolling Stones and this is what inspired the song. What is more likely is that he was bemused by shifting values of reality and unreality in the pop world, and liked the idea of lines about identity crises that contradicted each other. In America the 'controversial' line "I look all white but my Dad was black" was changed to "I try walking forward but my feet walk back", which reflects America's over-reaction to potentially sensitive comments on racial matters at this time.

Aside from its musical values – and the fact that it was the first record that Pete Townshend had ever produced himself – 'Substitute' has an interesting history as a single. It was released three times in the UK in March 1966, with a different B-side each time (although two of the B-sides were the same song with a different title). The third version contained on its B-side an instrumental entitled 'Waltz For A Pig' by 'The Who Orchestra' which was actually The Graham Bond Organisation. This was the most public manifestation of the Shel Talmy (aka the pig!) problem.

It reached number 5 in the UK charts but flopped in the US where it became the only Who single to be issued through Atlantic Records, on their down market Atco subsidiary.

I'M A BOY

'I'm A Boy' was originally written as part of a longer project called Quads, a Townshend tale set in the future when parents could choose the sex of their children. The family in the story requests four girls but get three girls and a boy, and this single is the boy's lament at the error. Well advanced for its time, and with lyrics quite unlike anything anyone else was writing, it tips its hat to The Beach Boys with its high harmonies, but the great counterpoint between guitar and drums is 100% Who..

The Who recorded two versions of this song, one of which was released as a single in August of 1966. This is the second version which features John on French horn.

In a seemingly endless programme of reissues, occasionally timed to appear when The Who went out on tour, five other major retrospectives of The Who have been released by either MCA or Polydor. All tracks on these albums have been covered in detail above.

THE STORY OF THE WHO
POLYDOR 2683 069, RELEASED SEPTEMBER 1976 (UK ONLY)

Magic Bus, Substitute, Boris The Spider, Run Run Run, I'm A Boy, Heatwave, My Generation (edit from 'Live At Leeds), Pictures Of Lily, Happy Jack, The Seeker, I Can See For Miles, Bargain, Squeeze Box, Amazing Journey, Acid Queen, Do You Think It's Alright, Fiddle About, Pinball Wizard, I'm Free, Tommy's Holiday Camp, We're Not Gonna Take It, Summertime Blues (edit from 'Leeds'), Baba O'Riley, Behind Blue Eyes, Slip Kid, Won't Get Fooled Again.

HOOLIGANS
MCA2 12001, RELEASED OCTOBER 1981 (US ONLY)

I Can't Explain, I Can See For Miles, Pinball Wizard, Let's See Action, Summertime Blues (from 'Leeds'), Relay, Baba O'Riley, Behind Blue Eyes, Bargain, Song Is Over, Join Together, Squeeze Box, Slip Kid, The Real Me, 5.15, Drowned, Had Enough, Sister Disco, Who Are You.

THE WHO COLLECTION
IMCD4 1/IMCD4 2; RELEASED OCTOBER 1985 (UK ONLY)

Volume 1: I Can't Explain, Anyway, Anyhow Anywhere, My Generation, Substitute, A Legal Matter, The Kids Are Alright, I'm A Boy, Happy Jack, Boris The Spider, Pictures Of Lily, I Can See For Miles, Won't Get Fooled Again, The Seeker, Let's See Action, Join Together, Relay, Love Reign O'er Me, Squeeze Box;
Volume 2: Who Are You, Long Live Rock, 5.15, You Better You Bet, Magic Bus, Summertime Blues, Shaking All

Over, Pinball Wizard, The Acid Queen, I'm Free, We're Not Gonna Take It, Baba O'Riley, Behind Blue Eyes, Bargain.

THE SINGLES
UK: POLYDOR WHOD 17 (UK ONLY), RELEASED NOVEMBER 1984; CD: 815 965-2

Substitute, I'm A Boy, Happy Jack, Pictures Of Lily, I Can See For Miles, Magic Bus, Pinball Wizard, My Generation, Summertime Blues, Won't Get Fooled Again, Let's See Action, Join Together, Squeeze Box, Who Are You, You Better You Bet.

WHO'S BETTER WHO'S BEST
UK: POLYDOR 835 389-1/2, RELEASED MARCH 1988; US: MCA2 8031

My Generation, Anyway Anyhow Anywhere, The Kids Are Alright, Substitute, I'm A Boy, Happy Jack, Pictures Of Lily, I Can See For Miles, Who Are You, Won't Get Fooled Again, Magic Bus, I Can't Explain, Pinball Wizard, I'm Free, See Me Feel Me,

Squeeze Box, Join Together, You Better You Bet, Baba O'Riley.

'Who's Better Who's Best', with interesting booklet notes by Richard Barnes, the writer and close friend of Pete Townshend, had become the standard Who 'Greatest Hits' collection in most territories at the time of writing. However, the quality of the mastering is far inferior to that on '30 Years Of Maximum R&B' (see below), and those seeking out a single CD of Who hits are advised to hang on to their money until the newly re-mixed and remastered tracks of the band's best known songs (as used on 'Maximum R&B') are collected on to a single CD. This ought to occur before the end of 1995.

COMPILATIONS OF RARE MATERIAL

In an attempt to 'tidy up' The Who's back catalogue Polydor issued two albums of 'Rarities' – mostly obscure B-sides – during the Eighties. Both volumes have now been compiled on to one budget-priced CD [Polydor 847 670 - 2]. In a similar move, MCA issued two albums entitled 'Who's Missing' and 'Two's Missing', both of which contained more interesting track selections than their UK counterparts. Unlike the UK 'Rarities', the MCA albums offered some material not previously available on official releases anywhere in the world, as well as material not previously available in the US except on import.

RARITIES VOL 1 1966-69
UK: POLYDOR SPELP 9

CIRCLES
(aka INSTANT PARTY)

'Circles' has a strange pedigree as far as release goes. Produced by Shel Talmy, it first appeared as the B-side of 'Substitute'; then, retitled 'Instant Party' and produced by The Who, as the B-side of the next pressing of 'Substitute' because Talmy injuncted the first pressing. Then Talmy plonked his production of it on the back of 'A Legal Matter' which he released as a single without The

Who's consent. This version, which can be found on the US 'My Generation' album and is the superior of the two, contains a chaotic guitar solo two years ahead of its time. Unfortunately but inevitably, the version on 'Rarities 1' is the inferior re-recording.

Either way, it's one of Pete's best 1966 shots with another of his slash chord solos backed up with thundering drums, and John's French horn on the fade out; less appealing than The Who's 'genuine' singles of the era but still quirky enough to warrant repeated listening and an excellent B-side.

DISGUISES

A poor mix of the best track on 'Ready, Steady Who', a brief attempt by The Who to move in the psychedelic direction that The Beatles were taking on their 'Rubber Soul' and 'Revolver' LPs. The production is denser than any other Who record up to this time, with a guitar clanging like hammer against anvil, and the subject matter decidedly bizarre for what appears at first glance to be a love song.

BATMAN
(Hefti)

A largely instrumental version of the theme from the *Batman* TV series, played with verve and competence but eminently forgettable.

BUCKET T
(Altfield, Christian, Torrence)

The first track on Side one of their EP 'Ready Steady Who' is The Who's stab at an unremarkable Jan and Dean car song featuring Keith on reasonably well pitched high falsetto lead vocals. Although it was a surprise hit in Sweden of all places – blondes the world over must like surf music – it was rather slight and nowhere near as impressive as the much denser 'Disguises' which opens Side two of the EP.

BARBARA ANN
(Fassert)

Surrendering to Keith's fondness for surf music, The Who do their best with The Beach Boys' noted rocker, but try as they might it's hardly their forté, and Keith's vocals can't match those of his Californian idols. The highlight is Pete's throw-away solo.

IN THE CITY
(Moon, Entwistle)

Bottom heavy but reasonably accurate Beach Boys pastiche, this time featuring just Moon and Entwistle, who apparently didn't tell the other two they were recording, and suffering as a result, especially in the vocal department. B-side of 'I'm A Boy'.

I'VE BEEN AWAY
(Entwistle)

A most un-Who like country and western song which meanders along to little purpose with amusing lyrics about feuding brothers, jail terms, and vengeance. As lightweight as The Who ever got in the Sixties. B-side of 'Happy Jack'.

DOCTOR DOCTOR
(Entwistle)

One of John's best ever Sixties songs with the composer singing a series of mildly amusing lines about his various illnesses in a very high-pitched voice to a catchy rock melody. This would have been regarded as a novelty song were it not for the enthusiastic, fast paced backing track. B-side of 'Pictures Of Lily'.

THE LAST TIME

When Mick Jagger and Keith Richards were jailed on drug charges in 1967, The Who decided to offer their support by recording this track and 'Under My Thumb' as a single and bung it out *tout de suite*. Apparently it was their intention to record one Stones track a month until The Glimmer Twins were released but fortunately for all concerned, the errant Stones were sprung before The Who got around to recording 'Satisfaction'. A good job too... The Who's effort is workmanlike but despite an upward key change towards the end, lacks both the attack and the menace of the Stones. Pete played bass because John was away on his honeymoon, aboard the QEll.

UNDER MY THUMB
(Jagger, Richards)

The second Stones cover essayed by The Who after Mick and Keith were jailed for drug offences. The vocals are weak but the catchy little riff is intact, and Pete's fuzz box solo almost makes the effort worthwhile. As on 'The Last Time', Pete played bass. For collectors only.

SOMEONE'S COMING
(Entwistle)

Mexican trumpets herald Roger's first ever stab at a song written by John, this one a mildly-diverting but essentially lightweight pop song with lyrics in the 'Wake Up Little Suzie' mode. B-side of UK 'I Can See For Miles'.

MARY ANNE WITH THE SHAKY HAND(S)

A completely different recording of the song that appeared on 'The Who Sell Out'. This version, with electric guitar dominant, features Roger's voice through a tremolo effect to give that s-h-a-k-y sound, and there's an understated organ solo. Lacking the bounce of the acoustic version, it was used as the B-side of the US single of 'I Can See For Miles'.

DOGS

A contender for the strangest single The Who ever released, 'Dogs' is clearly influenced by the Cockney rock style of The Small Faces on 'Lazy Sunday Afternoon', or even Ray Davies' eccentric Englishness which resulted in so many great Kinks songs. It's a strange, quite complex song, about the British working class male's love of greyhound racing and beer, almost comic but with just the right amount of Who-like influences and performance to suggest that they really meant it. The closing vocal 'armonies are quite luvverly.

CALL ME LIGHTNING

'Call Me Lightning' was one of the first songs written by Pete Townshend, around the same time as 'I Can't Explain', and was even suggested for their first single. Its mildly funky R&B feel is emphasised by chanted doo-wop backing vocals and John's bass solo, with Roger emoting as best he could on lyrics that no-one bar Pete understood. John gets a bass solo towards the end.

Pete: "It tries to be a slightly surly Jan and Dean king of song to satisfy Keith and John's then interest in surf music, which I thought was going to be a real problem. Being a trumped up Mod band was bad enough for us to handle, but trying to be a trumped-up Mod band playing R&B music with surf overtones was almost impossible... this song was trying to be all things to all men."

In the UK 'Lightning' was the B-side of 'Dogs' but in the US it was a 1968 single in its own right and reached number 40.

DR JEKYLL AND MR HYDE
(Entwistle)

John's attempt to translate Hammer horror into his music succeeds admirably, with a scarey opening, menacing bass line and spooky French horn solo. Indeed, John's bass carries the melody and, at the climax, he manages both a wicked scream and a rather macabre growl. A novelty item. B-side of 'Magic Bus'.

RARITIES VOL 2
POLYDOR SPELP 10

JOIN TOGETHER

Opening with Roger on Jew's harp and harmonica, or possibly Pete on synthesizer reproducing the sound of a Jew's harp, 'Join Together' was a key song in 'Lifehouse' which expresses Pete's ultimate fantasy of band and audience becoming one. Although – like its companion piece 'Let's See Action' – its rhythms bear little relation to the power chord style normally projected by The Who, the band play it quite superbly, jostling together with effortless syncopation. 'Join Together' was issued as a single in 1972 and it reached number nine in the charts.

I DON'T KNOW MYSELF

A 'Lifehouse' reject which wasn't quite up to the standard of the other songs Pete was writing in 1970, 'I Don't Know Myself' blends a fierce verse and chorus with a strange, country and western style middle eight which features Keith tapping a wooden block. Often played live around the end of the Sixties, but dropped when 'Who's Next' provided the band with better stage material. Used as the B-side of 'Won't Get Fooled Again' single.

HEAVEN AND HELL
(Entwistle)

Although never recorded to John or The Who's ultimate satisfaction, 'Heaven And Hell' was one of the greatest songs that John Entwistle contributed to The Who's live set, a harsh warning about the perils of mortal misbehaviour which rocked along as well as anything Pete was writing at the time. 'Heaven And Hell' was frequently used to open Who sets during the late Sixties when 'Tommy' got a full airing, and it allowed Pete plenty of opportunity to stretch out on the solo. First released as the B-side of the single edit of 'Summertime Blues'.

WHEN I WAS A BOY
(Entwistle)

A tastefully arranged brass band introduction sets the mood for John's nostalgic song about age and disillusionment. More sincere than is usual for Entwistle, 'When I Was A Boy' was originally intended for 'Lifehouse', and its straining tempo maintains the interest throughout. Definitely one of John's better Who songs, though the production is weak. B-side of 'Let's See Action'.

LET'S SEE ACTION

A call to arms and another uncharacteristic single from the early Seventies, 'Let's See Action' has an almost folksy feel, although a trilling piano carries the slight, rather laborious melody and the song is over-long. The contrast between Roger's determined vocal and Pete's more introspective middle-eight intrusion is both assured and re-assuring. It wasn't a hit (briefly it reached number 16) but The Who hadn't lost their way: Pete was just experimenting in order to avoid stagnation.

RELAY

Wah-wah guitar, or 'treated synthesizer guitar', opens a full-tilt rocker about the need to exchange ideas and information or at least pass them on to the next generation. With a ringing acoustic guitar in one channel and the wah-wah in the other, not to mention John's exemplary bass playing high up the fretboard, there's a wealth of good ideas, both musical and lyrical, here; also, a nice allegory about passing on the baton in a relay race. Far too weighty as a single, it reached number 21 in 1973.

WASPMAN
(Moon)

Three minutes of pure lunacy allegedly originated by Keith during a long and boring flight across Australia when he adopted the guise of a wasp and ran around the plane making buzzing noises with a groupie's bra wrapped around his face. The Who never went back to Australia afterwards.

Relocated to the recording studio Keith continues to buzz while the band play a truly monotonous three chord riff, and it would be generous to describe the result as filler material. On other instrumentals credited to Keith in the past he'd made a point of doing something special on the drums, but not this time alas. Risible, really. B-side of 'Relay' single.

HERE FOR MORE
(Daltrey)

Roger's second solo composing credit in The Who's catalogue – the first was 'See My Way' back in 1966 – is a fairly lightweight country and western style song without The Who's normal attack which probably means that Keith was absent from the session. Despite its authentic country licks and lap-steel guitar, The Who were never in danger of becoming The Eagles, for which we can all be thankful. It was used as the B-side of 'The Seeker'.

WATER

An overlong, rather heavy-handed rocker dating from the late Sixties, 'Water' is another 'Lifehouse' reject, this one mixing a rather lascivious hook line ('water' rhymes with 'daughter' throughout) into a song in which 'water' becomes an allegory for quenching spiritual thirst. It was played live quite often in the late Sixties/early Seventies and seemed set for inclusion on whatever album that would follow 'Leeds'. Eventually Pete came up with the several far better songs, and 'Water' was consigned to the scrap heap, only to resurface as the B-side of '5.15' in 1973.

BABY DON'T YOU DO IT

(Holland, Dozier, Holland)

Probably recorded live at the San Francisco Civic on December 12, 1971, this is a fierce work-out of the Tamla song made famous by Marvin Gaye, highlighted by Keith's energetic drumming, Roger's strident vocals and The Who's unique ability to turn soul into furious rock at the drop of a hat. With the band on the same form as they were the night they recorded 'Live At Leeds', this track presents The Who at their live best, playing off one another as no other band could, with each outstanding individually as well. There's some lovely bass work, and Pete's buzz-saw guitar solo towards the end is terrific. During the furious 'head for home' climax Pete, John and Keith play their hearts out with Roger hollering to be heard above the din. Then, just to stress the point, there's a false ending and the band rev up yet again.

The Who often played this song live during 1971 but abandoned it because the songs from 'Who's Next' offered them a wider choice of quality material. B-side of the 'Join Together' single.

WHO'S MISSING

US: MCA 5641, RELEASED NOVEMBER, 1985;
CD: MCA MCAD-31221

Full track listing: Leaving Here, Lubie, Shout And Shimmy, Anytime You Want Me, Barbara Ann, I'm A Boy (alternate take), Mary Anne With The Shaky Hands (sic) (electric version), Heaven And Hell, Here For More, I Don't Even Know Myself, When I Was A Boy, Bargain (live).

Tracks not dealt with above are as follows:

LEAVING HERE
(Holland/Dozier/Holland)

A previously unreleased High Numbers out take and the toughest of the four HN recordings extant, 'Leaving Here' was originally a minor hit for Tamla writer Eddie Holland. Though Roger's vocals sound strained, the band play in the powerful, unrestrained manner which would soon become their trademark. As in all the HN tracks, the drums are recorded too low.

LUBIE
(Revere, Lindsay)

Unsophisticated beat boom era rock from The Who before they'd settled on the style they made their own. Probably recorded for 'My Generation' but dropped in favour of Townshend originals.

SHOUT AND SHIMMY
(Brown)

With their ability to turn soul into rock at the drop of a drumstick, 'Shout And Shimmy' became a passionate live workout, the first in a series of drum vocal duels that reached its apotheosis in 'Young Man Blues'. This version, used as the B-side of 'My Generation', is energetic enough, but check out the live version on 'The Kids Are Alright' video on which Keith *is* The Who, and the other three are mere bystanders.

ANY TIME YOU WANT ME
(Ragavoy, Mimms)

A slowish beat ballad with soul overtones

on which Roger tries to emulate the sound of John Lennon on The Beatles' first LP. Simple, melodic and with a nice piano track from Nicky Hopkins, it features some early Townshend background vocals – 'Ooh, Ooh' style – and was used as the B-side to 'Anyway Anyhow Anywhere' in the US.

BARGAIN

The Who live at their very best... taken from the show recorded at San Francisco on December 12, 1971 (see 'Baby Don't You Do It', above) when they were at their height as a live band. Incorporates a false ending, thumping coda and *blitzkrieg* climax. Also included on '30 Years Of Maximum R&B' (see below).

TWO'S MISSING
US: MCA 5712, RELEASED APRIL 1987;
CD: MCA MCAD-31222

Full track listing: Bald Headed Woman, Under My Thumb, My Wife (live, San Francisco), I'm A Man, Dogs, Dogs II,

Circles, The Last Time, Water, Daddy Rolling Stone, Heatwave (alternate take), Going Down (live), Motoring, Waspman.

Tracks not dealt with above are as follows:

BALD HEADED WOMAN
(Talmy)

A *very* short harmonica based slow and moody blues song 'written' by Shel Talmy and used by him as the B-side of 'I Can't Explain', a common practice at the time which ensured that the producer would earn publishing royalties from sales if the A-side was a hit (which it was). Features Jimmy Page on fuzz-box lead guitar but poor young Keith is mixed far too low.

DOGS PART II
(Moon, Towser, Jason)

This is a power-packed instrumental jam, led from the front, back and sides by Keith doing what he did best: pounding his heart out on the skins. Keith, John and Pete all take solos in a frenzied, garage band style rave-up. Probably the nearest thing to a Keith Moon drum solo in the entire Who catalogue, this track was the B-side of 'Pinball Wizard' and, as such, would have earned its composers a tidy sum in royalties: one can only ponder how Towser and Jason, Pete and John's pet dogs respectively, spent their cash.

DADDY ROLLING STONE
(Mason)

A fierce blues workout, with Roger especially in pit-bull frame of mind, captured by producer Shel Talmy and probably destined for The Who's first album until Pete came up with a surfeit of original songs. Occasionally played live, briefly, during Pete's leaps into the unknown. Originally released as the B-side of 'Anyway Anyhow Anywhere' but not available in the US until the release of this album.

GOING DOWN
(Freddie King)

Recorded live at San Francisco, this is a slow but heavy blues jam on a Freddie King song with negligible vocals, typical of how The Who might stretch the climax of any number of songs in their catalogue, depending on their mood on the night. Pete's guitar dominates, but John and Keith provide him with a superb platform.

MOTORING
(Holland/Dozier/Holland)

A Martha Reeves and The Vandellas song recorded by The Who in 1965 with Shel Talmy producing which was intended for their first LP but pushed aside when Pete came up with better material. Not one of the band's better early efforts but the playing is disciplined and towards the end there is another early example of the drum and vocal exchanges that Keith and Roger would eventually perfect.

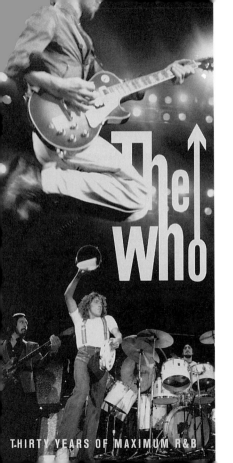

30 YEARS OF MAXIMUM R&B

UK: POLYDOR 521 751-2, RELEASED JULY 1994;
US: MCA MCAD4-11020.

In July of 1994 The Who released a four CD box set (also a 4-cassette version in the US) containing all their best known work, several rarities and a number of previously unreleased recordings. Many of the tracks were punctuated by soundbites – the group talking amongst themselves in the studio, Pete making announcements from the stage or Keith telling jokes – and the package included a sumptuous 72-page full colour booklet with essays by Pete Townshend, Keith Altham and Dave Marsh. It also included a comprehensive Who chronology, a discography by Who archivist Ed Hanel and credits that gave an abundance of recording details not previously available.

Most of the 79 tracks, bar those recorded with Shel Talmy, were remastered and/or remixed and the sound quality is uniformly excellent. This is especially noticeable on the four songs by The Who as The High Numbers and the tracks produced by Kit Lambert in the Sixties. Even without access to the master tapes the Talmy recordings have been tidied up as best they can by co-producer Jon Astley, who co-produced 'Who Are You' with Glyn Johns and who is also Pete's brother-in-law.

The package was very well received by critics. *Q* magazine in the UK gave it a maximum five star rating and described it as the best box set ever produced by anybody; similarly, *Rolling Stone* magazine in the US gave it a maximum five stars too. The most common criticism was the omission of the original 'Substitute' in favour of the version recorded live at Leeds; other critics felt that the post-Keith Moon era was under represented, though the compilers were all of the opinion that the *real* Who existed only while Keith was

alive, and that his drumming was such an essential part of The Who's music that scant attention should be paid to the post-Moon era. Only six tracks out of 79 don't feature Keith.

In a short essay at the end of the booklet the compilers explain their reasons for including certain tracks and for excluding others. The full track listing is as follows:

CD 1: Pete dialogue*†; I'm The Face; Here 'Tis*; Zoot Suit; Leaving Here; I Can't Explain; Anyway, Anyhow, Anywhere; Daddy Rolling Stone; My Generation; The Kids Are Alright; The Ox; A Legal Matter; Pete dialogue*; Substitute†; I'm A Boy; Disguises; Happy Jack Jingle*; Happy Jack; Boris The Spider; So Sad About Us; A Quick One†; Pictures Of Lily; Early Morning Cold Taxi*; Coke 2*; (This Could Be) The Last Time; Can't Reach You; Girl's Eyes*; Bag O'Nails*; Call Me Lightning;
CD 2: Rotosound Strings; I Can See For Miles; Mary Anne With The Shaky Hand; Armenia City In The Sky; Tattoo; Our Love Was; Rael 1; Rael 2*; Track

Records*/Premier Drums; Sunrise; Jaguar*; Melancholia*; Fortune Teller*; Magic Bus; Little Billy; Russell Harty dialogue*†; Dogs; Overture; Acid Queen; Abbie Hoffman Incident*†; Underture†; Pinball Wizard; I'm Free; See Me, Feel Me*†; Heaven And Hell; Pete dialogue*; Young Man Blues†; Summertime Blues†; **CD 3:** Shaking All Over†; Baba O'Riley; Bargain†; Pure And Easy; The Song Is Over; Studio dialogue*†; Behind Blue Eyes; Won't Get Fooled Again; The Seeker (edit); Bony Moronie†; Let's See Action; Join Together; Relay; The Real Me*; 5.15 (single mix); Bell Boy; Love Reign O'er Me;
CD 4: Long Live Rock; Life With The Moons*; Naked Eye*†; University Challenge*; Slip Kid; Poetry Cornered*; Dreaming From The Waist*†; Blue Red And Grey; Life With The Moons 2*; Squeeze Box; My Wife*†; Who Are You; Music Must Change; Sister Disco; Guitar And Pen; You Better You Bet; Eminence Front; Twist And Shout*†; I'm A Man*†; Pete dialogue*†; Saturday Night's Alright For Fighting.

* Indicates recording previously unreleased or unavailable in this version.
† Indicates live recording.

The following tracks that appear on 'Maximum R&B' have not previously been dealt with in this analysis:

HERE 'TIS
(Ellis McDaniel)

A previously unreleased recording of The High Numbers playing a song by Bo Diddley that was a fixture in their 1964 live act. Nice harmony singing and guitar fills, with the beat carried by maracas. Simple but enjoyable.

EARLY MORNING COLD TAXI
(Daltrey, Langston)

An obscure outtake from 'Sell Out', previously unreleased but known to collectors for years, 'Taxi' is a straight pop song written by Roger and Who roadie Cyrano Langston, and is definitely Roger's best composition in The Who's catalogue.

GIRL'S EYES
(Moon)

There *was* a soft, sentimental side to Keith Moon, as this outtake demonstrates. After a typically Moon-like false start, it's a psychedelic folk-song, of sorts, that could have been written by Donovan, or even Syd Barrett. Gentle acoustic strumming shuffles things along and Pete closes the proceedings with what was probably the first and only take of his Spanish guitar style soloing. Utterly charming.

RAEL 2

A brief, plaintive coda to Rael proper, featuring Pete on solo piano and dirge-like vocals. A bit like a psalm.

JAGUAR

Astonishing drums lead into one of the heaviest tracks The Who ever recorded. The vocals may have been added as an afterthought, for it's the instrumental work, like that on 'The Ox', that carries a song whose lyrics could be obliquely influenced by either the cars or the animal.

MELANCHOLIA

Another 'Sell Out' outtake, 'Melancholia' is a curiously cold and cheerless but nevertheless powerful song taken at a slow, forced tempo which contrasts markedly with the style of music The Who were otherwise producing at the time.

FORTUNE TELLER
(Neville)

Benny Spellman's hit 'Fortune Teller', also covered by The Rolling Stones, was a staple of The Who's live act between 1968 and 1970. This lively studio version, recorded that year, remained unreleased until the box set came out.

ABBIE HOFFMAN INCIDENT

Just before The Who launched into 'Acid Queen' during their rendering of 'Tommy' at Woodstock on August 17, 1969, the late yippie politico Abbie Hoffman walked on stage and began to declaim the festival through Pete's mike. Pete yelled a few imprecations then unceremoniously booted him off stage. Although Pete later regretted his hasty action, the incident is part of Who folk-lore and is preserved for eternity here.

SEE ME FEEL ME

A forceful live version of the climax to 'Tommy' recorded live at Leeds University during the same show that produced The Who's 'Live At Leeds' album. The 'See Me Feel Me' introduction is actually taken from the studio recording, apart from the final refrain, because Roger sang this section off key on the night.

THE REAL ME

A previously unreleased reworking of the 'Quadrophenia' song taken from the audition for Kenney Jones at Ramport Studios, London, in January 1979.

LIFE WITH THE MOONS 1&2, UNIVERSITY CHALLENGE, POETRY CORNERED
(Moon)

Four set piece comedy items from Keith.

DREAMING FROM THE WAIST

A previously unreleased version recorded live at Swansea Football Ground on June 12, 1976, this was included simply because The Who performed the song faultlessly, especially the vocal harmonies on the verses, and because of John's immaculate bass solo towards the end which gained enormously when played live.

BONY MORONIE
(Williams)

A ragged but entertaining blast through the rock'n'roll standard recorded live at London's Young Vic during rehearsals for 'Lifehouse' in early 1971. Pete's guitar lacks precision and Keith sometimes isn't quite sure where to go next, but John's sturdy bass holds things together and

Roger, ever at home on an old rocker, gives a truly great vocal performance. The Who as a bar band, and definitely worth two quid on the door.

MY WIFE
(Entwistle)

A blistering version of John's 'My Wife' from the same gig as 'Dreaming From The Waist' (see above).

TWIST AND SHOUT
(Medley/Burns)

The Who frequently ended their 1982 shows with a full tilt version of 'Twist And Shout' in a similar arrangement to The Beatles' version on their 'Please Please Me' album which in turn was a re-reading of the version by The Isley Brothers. John Entwistle takes lead vocals because Roger couldn't reach high enough, but he's no John Lennon. Fun but certainly not essential.

I'M A MAN
(McDaniel)

A long reading of the Bo Diddley stomper first released by The Who way back in 1965 on their début album, and taken from the 1989 reunion tour with a cast of thousands. Roger over-eggs the pudding a bit with his appeals for crowd participation, but there's no denying the enthusiasm of the audience – and the band – even at this late stage in their career. This track did not appear on 'Join Together', the official album of the 1989 tour.

SATURDAY NIGHT'S ALRIGHT FOR FIGHTING
(John, Taupin)

The Who recorded Elton John's 'Saturday Night's Alright For Fighting' for a tribute album of Elton John/Bernie Taupin compositions entitled 'Two Rooms' which was released in 1991 and also featured Joe Cocker, Kate Bush, Sting, George Michael and many others. With Jon Astley on drums, Pete, Roger and John make the song their own, and segue neatly into Pete singing 'Border Song' half way through, thus bringing out the contrast between Roger and Pete's voices as in days of old.

AND FINALLY...

A recording of 'Tommy' by The London Symphony Orchestra and Chamber Choir (UK: ODE SP 88 001; US: ODE SP 99 001) was released worldwide towards the end of 1972. This was produced by the late Lou Reizner and featured Pete Townshend, Roger Daltrey and John Entwistle among an all star cast that also included Sandy Denny, Steve Winwood, Ringo Starr and Rod Stewart. It has subsequently been released on CD by Castle Communications.

Live recordings by The Who *not* found within The Who's own catalogue appear on the following albums:

WOODSTOCK (Atlantic 2663 001, released 1969; reissue K60001): We're Not Gonna Take It.

CONCERTS FOR THE PEOPLE OF KAMPUCHEA (Atlantic K60153, released March 1981): Baba O'Riley, Sister Disco, Behind Blue Eyes, See Me Feel Me.

THE MONTEREY INTERNATIONAL POP FESTIVAL (Rhino Records R270596, released 1993): Substitute, Summertime Blues, Pictures Of Lily, A Quick One, Happy Jack, My Generation (their entire 25 minute set).

Two songs credited to The Who with Simon Phillips on drums can be found on Pete Townshend's 'Iron Man' LP (Virgin CDV 2592, released March 1991):

FIRE
(Brown, Crane, Ker, Finesilver)
The Who seem quite at home on their radical re-write of one-time Track label-

mate Arthur Brown's 1968 chart topper, though there's little similarity between The Who and Brown. Lacking the terror-filled passion of Arthur Brown's version, The Who use a synthesizer backdrop and build up to an almost 'Day In The Life' style crescendo.

DIG

Featured live during the 1989 reunion tour because Pete was ostensibly promoting his 'Iron Man' album at the time, 'Dig' rolls along at a relaxed country pace, and features a deep voiced Roger and jangly style guitar solo. The repeated refrain "The old ones have seen two wars" at the end of each verse has a nice poignancy.

... and, just for the record, the only officially released songs *credited* to The Who that are not available on any album in either the UK or the US at the time of writing are the studio version of 'Young Man Blues' which appeared on a Track sampler LP called 'The House That Track Built' in 1969, and their cover of Martha And The Vandellas' 'Dancing In The Street', recorded live at the Philadelphia Spectrum on December 13, 1979, which appeared as an extra track on a CD re-issue of 'Won't Get Fooled Again' in June 1988.

VIDEOS

More than any other acts of their era, The Who were receptive to film cameras. Early managers Kit Lambert and Chris Stamp came from a film background and weren't slow to realise the promotional advantage of film, and for this reason there is probably more footage of The Who kicking around than any of their contemporaries from the Sixties *and* Seventies.

It would be interesting to speculate on how Lambert and Stamp would operate in the current era, when a video is a virtual necessity for any band with serious chart aspirations. Their initial attraction to The Who came about largely through their appreciation of the group's visual appeal, which they sought to enhance with lights and mayhem, and they were among the first to film performance footage of a rock band purely for promotional use. Their legacy is three lengthy Who videos containing far more live and lip-sync footage than The Beatles

and Rolling Stones have been able to muster between them.

At the time of writing there are five Who videos on the market, and the band can also be seen in the movie *Woodstock* (and heard in *Quadrophenia*).

THE KIDS ARE ALRIGHT
(Spectrum 791 514 2)

A first-rate 100 minute documentary on The Who which, because it was issued in 1979, appears almost as a tribute to Keith Moon. Includes live footage, lip-sync footage and interviews stretching back to 1964 and concluding with specially filmed performances of 'Baba O'Riley' and 'Won't Get Fooled Again' in 1978. Highlights include footage from *Woodstock* ('Pinball Wizard', 'Sparks' and 'See Me Feel Me') though the camera focuses primarily on Roger to the detriment of the rest of the band, the second half of 'A Quick One' from The Rolling Stones' *Rock & Roll Circus*, and the specially filmed 'Baba' and 'Fooled Again'. There are some amusing and insightful interviews with Pete stretching

THE WHO : VIDEOS

back to 1966 and spectacular footage of the band smashing their equipment, notably the opening sequence from The Smothers Brothers TV show in 1967. Also worth a mention is the non-performance b&w promo film made by The Who for 'Happy Jack' in 1966. Whoever suggested that Queen's 'Bohemian Rhapsody' was 'the first ever pop video' needs their head examined.

All in all *Kids...* is a definitive Who documentary, put together with genuine affection for the band by US fan Jeff Stein, and originally screened in cinemas. Highly recommended.

THE WHO ROCKS AMERICA 1982
(CBS/FOX 6234-50)

A complete concert by The Who with Kenney Jones on drums and Tim Gorman on keyboards filmed not in America as the title implies but at Toronto Maple Leaf Gardens on December 17, 1982, during the band's first 'farewell tour' of North America. By anyone else's standards The Who were still a great rock band but compared to their sprightly early days, they were going through the motions by this time, banging out their hits and throwing in a few new songs to keep the record company happy. Pete doesn't so much look bored as resigned, and reproducing the agile athleticism of old seems now to be a great effort. Only Roger retains the enthusiasm of old, not that John *ever* betrayed his emotions on stage. For enthusiasts only.

WHO'S BETTER WHO'S BEST
(Channel 5 CFV 05562)

A collection of footage, live and lip-sync, of The Who performing their best known songs, marred by the inclusion of several clips that already appear in *The Kids Are Alright*. Not essential, although clips of 'The Kids Are Alright', 'I Can See For Miles' and the opening 'My Generation' are worth the price of admission. The clips for 'I'm Free' and 'Magic Bus' are unavailable elsewhere and the laser disc version features 'Relay' from The Russell Harty show which is also otherwise unobtainable.

LIVE TOMMY

(CMV Enterprises 49028 2)

A complete concert from the 1989 25th anniversary tour filmed at the Universal Amphitheater in Los Angeles on August 24. This particular show was a charity event in which several guest artists took part in 'Tommy' which occupies the entire first half of the video. They include Elton John, Phil Collins, Steve Winwood, Patti Labelle and Billy Idol. During the second half, the much augmented Who band run through a selection of hits. For enthusiasts only.

30 YEARS OF MAXIMUM R&B LIVE

(PolyGram Video 631 012-3)

A fine companion to *The Kids Are Alright* and The Who's box set, '30 Years' presents two and a half hours of genuine live performances by The Who arranged chronologically and punctuated by 1994 interviews with Pete, Roger and John in which they talk about The Who's career, with particular emphasis on the development of their stage work. Considering the amount of footage already on *Kids*, producer Nick Ryle did an outstanding job researching all this 'new' footage, none of which was on 'Kids' or had been available commercially prior to this release.

Among the many highlights are two numbers from The Who's Isle Of Wight set in 1970 ('Young Man Blues' and 'Don't Even Know Myself'), four from their massive open air gig at Charlton Football Ground in 1974 ('Substitute', 'Drowned', 'Bell Boy' and 'My Generation') and a snappy 'Happy Jack' from the London Coliseum in 1969 with Keith at his very, very best.

The first 90 minutes feature the band with Keith on drums; thereafter it's Kenney Jones and, at the very end, The Who plus the touring ensemble that gathered for their 1989 25th anniversary tour.

Also included in the package are excellent liner notes by John Atkins, including precise details about the origins of the clips.

Highly recommended.

INDEX

Bold page numbers indicate a descriptive entry.

6/97(27964)